f**P**

MUCH ADO ABOUT LOVING

What Our Favorite Novels Can Teach You About
Date Expectations, Not-So-Great Gatsbys,
and Love in the Time of Internet Personals

Jack Murnighan
and Maura Kelly

FREE PRESS

New York London Toronto Sydney New Delhi

Free Press
A Division of Simon & Schuster, Inc.
1230 Avenue of the Americas
New York, NY 10020

First Free Press hardcover edition January 2012

FREE PRESS and colophon are trademarks of Simon & Schuster, Inc.

For information about special discounts for bulk purchases, please contact
Simon & Schuster Special Sales at 1-866-506-1949
or business@simonandschuster.com.

The Simon & Schuster Speakers Bureau can bring authors to your live event.
For more information or to book an event contact the
Simon & Schuster Speakers Bureau at 1-866-248-3049 or
visit our website at www.simonspeakers.com.

Designed by Ruth Lee-Mui

Manufactured in the United States of America

1 3 5 7 9 10 8 6 4 2

Library of Congress Cataloging-in-Publication Data
Murnighan, Jack.
Much ado about loving : what our favorite novels can teach you about date expectations,
not-so-great Gatsbys, and love in the time of Internet personals /
by Jack Murnighan & Maura Kelly.
p. cm.
1. Man-woman relationships. 2. Dating (Social customs). 3. Man-woman
relationships in literature. 4. Dating (Social customs) in literature. 5. Courtship in
literature. I. Kelly, Maura. II. Title.
HQ801.M846 2012
306.73'4—dc23 2011024156

ISBN 978-1-4516-2124-2
ISBN 978-1-4516-2126-6 (ebook)

NOTE TO READER:
Names and identifying details of some of the people portrayed
in this book have been changed.

CONTENTS

Tragicomedy of Errors
Types to Watch Out For

The Taming of the . . . Who?
The Seduction Process

All's Well That Ends with an Orgasm
Ah, Yes, the Sex

Midsummer's (or Any Other Season's) Nightmare
Signs You Should Abandon Ship

Love's Labors Found
Making It Work

INTRODUCTION

Maura Kelly

I've made a living in a rather peculiar manner over the past few years: by writing about relationships. Unfortunately for me—but fortunately for my career—I always seemed to have a crazy new dating tale to tell. Like the one about the accomplished scientist who'd had a thick shaggy mane in every picture he'd posted online—though in person he was about 94 percent bald. We sat down to dinner at the nice restaurant where he'd invited me to dine, and he promptly ordered a *banana*, despite the fact that "individual pieces of fruit in phallic shapes" were not on the menu. "Charge me whatever you'd like!" he told the befuddled waitress. Come to think of it, that's more or less what he said to me when the check came. His exact words were: "We can split it, or I can pay, or *you* can pay." Never had I been given so many options. It was after we divvied it up that I made like a banana and split.

Or there's the story about the very tall young *gentleman*—I use that term loosely—who was studying for a PhD in economics at Columbia. Over tapas, he explained that he was kinda stalking another chick but went on to assure me that I had nothing to worry about—I wasn't pretty enough to make him crazy. I responded with typical unflappability: I locked myself in the bathroom for twenty minutes and sobbed.

There was also the dude I met up with in Prospect Park one summer, after we had a brief phone discussion about our lives and likes, including our favorite foods. He brought his guitar to the rendezvous and serenaded me with a song he'd written especially for the occasion.

It began: "Maura Kelly is a nutter . . . who likes peanut butter." That's probably as close to immortality in verse as I'll ever get.

Because of my unusual professional specialty, friends and strangers often seek out my advice—asking me about, say, how they should interpret not having heard from a date for a full twenty-four hours since their first hang-out session, how long they should wait before having sex with the person they've recently begun seeing, or how it might go over if they mention the recent passing of their beloved cat in their Internet dating profile. When this kind of thing first began to happen, it made me really nervous. I'm a *dating columnist*, after all—which is essentially the opposite of an expert on blissful romantic commitment! Could *I* really provide helpful counsel?

Heck, I was always turning to friends to ask how they thought I should handle the latest Lothario in my life. In particular, I sought out my cowriter Jack Murnighan. When he and I first got to know each other—after I was assigned to write a piece about his previous book for *The Daily Beast*—he dazzled me, and not only with his erudite yet engaging personality. There was, too, the thick gingery hair, the high cheekbones, the strong jaw, the wide smile full of perfect teeth, and enough lady-killing charm to fell an army of Amazons. As if that weren't enough, he could effortlessly quote from Proust or cite David Foster Wallace. Jack had spent the better part of his life extracting the wisdom from literature (majoring in philosophy and semiotics at Brown, getting a PhD in literature from Duke); he was an unusual mix of bookworm and pretty boy. Surprising, too, was how incredibly down-to-earth he was. In fact, there was so much to like about him that I was *relieved* to hear he had a girlfriend; that meant the question of his not being interested in me romantically was removed from the equation.

It began to happen that if I was in Jack's part of town, I'd swing by his apartment—a crow's nest of a one bedroom, perched high above Chinatown, lined wall to wall to wall with books; we'd make

some dinner, or have a little tea, and talk about our love lives. He always had the most satisfying takes on mine. Possibly that's because he'd once been a very scrawny and lonely boy, so he could relate to my fear that no one would ever understand the truth of my hopeful but hapless heart. Or maybe it had more to do with the fact that he read so much. He could empathize with certain female characters—like self-punishing Katerina from *The Brothers Karamazov* and underassertive Mrs. Ramsay from *To the Lighthouse*—as much as with me. And he'd gathered some great lessons from the brilliant psychologists who have written the world's great novels.

Not long after we became buddies, I stopped over to see Jack on my way home from a hotel-bar party in SoHo, thrown by the literary journal *Open City* to celebrate its latest issue. Not one guy had given me the time of day. Did my new black cocktail dress mean nothing to those louts? I was demoralized.

"Is there any way for me to become one of those chicks who casts a spell over every dude she meets?" I asked Jack. "Because there are some women who just—I don't know—they have that je ne sais quoi. They're not necessarily outstandingly gorgeous or brilliant or success-ful . . . but they know how to rock it."

When Jack stood up, I assumed he was going to make me a cup of tea while telling me I shouldn't let it bother me. Instead, he plucked an enormous slab of literary sustenance from his shelf and put it down in front of me: *War and Peace*.

"Read that," Jack said. "The character Natasha? She'll show you all you need to know about being alluring."

I frowned. "It's rather *long*, isn't it?"

"I thought you said *Bleak House* was one of your favorite novels. That's long, too."

"But it's also awesome."

Jack pointed at the cover. "You'll love this. You won't be able to put it down."

"I will when my arm starts cramping as I try to keep hold of it."

Despite my grousing, I started reading the book. I hadn't had an easy time getting into *Anna Karenina* but Tolstoy's other biggie sucked me right in; a vivid soap opera of love triangles, family dynamics, and bad matches, it deserved its reputation as the world's most beautifully told epic. But if there was anything particularly illuminating about the behavior of the main female character, Natasha, I'd missed it. She was basically just pretty, wasn't she? It wasn't like she was consciously *doing* anything to make herself more appealing. Right?

Jack was quick to correct my misreading. And once he'd explained Natasha's secret—read his chapter "Scorin' Piece" to find out what it is—I had an epiphany worthy of a lightning-struck religious convert.

Eureka!

Like that, I was more in control of my romantic destiny.

When I passed on Jack's instructions to one of my dearest friends, she grumbled, "It's not fair that you have Jack all to yourself."

I began to think maybe she was right. I began to think he should write a book about how serious reading can make us all smarter about relationships. And then it occurred to me that we should write it together . . .

That's how we ended up here.

In these pages, we'll be considering all kinds of romantic conundrums. Like the case of a young woman who was snubbed by a stuck-up rich kid because he thought her parents were too déclassé. We'll talk about a dude who just couldn't cure his infatuation with the prettiest girl in town, even though she wouldn't give him the time of day. We'll consider a girl who was in love with a guy whose mother was so jealous of her son's crush that she tried to break them up. And we'll look at a couple in a long-distance relationship who try to keep the flame alive by writing each other long notes—even though they've never had a meaningful face-to-face conversation.

Are you thinking that I'm conversant in such dramatics because my *friends* have been in predicaments like those I mentioned? It's a good guess, but the examples above were actually pulled from novels that have endured through the years: *Pride and Prejudice, Great Expectations, Sons and Lovers,* and *Love in the Time of Cholera,* respectively. Clearly, not much has changed through the centuries when it comes to romance.

Then again, plenty has. The Victorians, for instance, sure weren't discussing the statistical appeal of Internet dating sites (like 'em or not, they up your odds of meeting somebody cool), or trying to determine if a woman would blow her cachet if she pursued a relationship with the guy in her office, or trying to figure out how to handle "friendships with benefits." They didn't have to deal with all the strange, new-fangled, often painful methods we have for meeting people. (Speed dating? Ugh.) They had pretty strict dating mores that made things a lot less confusing (if also more constraining) than they are today. They didn't have the same kind of expectations that we do about finding the perfect partner—sexual dynamo, emotional stalwart, and best buddy all rolled into one.

Between all the pressure we put on ourselves to find a soul mate and all the possible ways to couple up, it's no wonder we single people are a little shell-shocked. It's not surprising that we're constantly fretting over our personal lives—trying to figure out if the ball is in our court after an ambiguous ending to a date, if we should compromise on that factor we thought was so essential in a mate, if we should swear off the head cases we always find ourselves attracted to . . . and all the rest.

Hoping to arrive at true love much sooner than later, we turn everywhere for answers: self-help books, daytime TV, magazines, radio talk shows, friends, relatives, and shrinks. But the *real* experts on love have been around for a while, as Jack and I have realized, and their insights ring true generation after generation. Part of the reason

the great novelists *are* so great is because of the timeless lessons they impart.

All the same, we understand that a large part of the reason more people don't read these books is because nobody has the time. That's why we did it for you; we went through some of our favorite classics, looking for clues that would help us solve today's romantic dilemmas.

But does our simply being voracious readers—and veterans of the dating scene—and people who've written extensively about our personal lives—mean you should listen to us? As I've indicated, I'm perennially single. And Jack has been engaged twice. We're not exactly the poster children for happy love lives. So . . . ?

I'm going to put off addressing the question of our expertise for another few moments while I ask you to consider the personal life of a certain female author, one whom gajillions of young women—and at least a few hundred young men—have turned to when looking for wisdom and solace about relationships. The novelist of whom I speak has served as inspiration for generations of sassy single girls. She was writing books that were essentially romantic comedies long before Renée Zellweger was born, let alone chosen to star in *Bridget Jones's Diary*; books in which the heroines, preoccupied with finding husbands, eventually end up with the right guys and live happily ever after. But the writer herself never married. The one and only time she was proposed to, she acted as one of her heroines might: She considered accepting the offer because the guy had lots of money— but turned him down because, from the sounds of things, he was an unbearable prig. When her young niece asked her for advice about a man she was thinking about marrying, the author wrote, "[I] entreat you not to commit yourself farther, & not to think of accepting him unless you really do like him. Anything is to be preferred or endured rather than marrying without Affection." One of her characters repeats her words almost exactly when talking to her sister Lizzy—the heroine in *Pride and Prejudice*. I'm talking about Jane Austen, of course.

Think about Tolstoy—a writer whose two most important novels are gorgeous meditations on how to find contentment in life and love even though by all accounts the man himself was a bitch of a husband. As his long-suffering wife wrote in her journal: "All the things that he preaches for the happiness of humanity only complicate life to the point where it becomes harder and harder for me to live . . . I devote so much love and care to him, and his heart is so icy."

Keep in mind, too, Charles Dickens, whose first-person narrators can be so self-deprecating, affectionate, and purehearted; whose wonderful stories about the redemptive power of love and kindness have helped me get through some of my, um, bleakest moments. The man left his wife in middle age—after they had ten children together—because he'd fallen in love with an eighteen-year-old girl!

So, yes: Dickens, Tolstoy, and Austen have provided me with great psychological knowledge—and yet they certainly struggled in their romantic lives, as I have. But they weren't asking us to behave as they did. They were asking us to observe their wonderfully, terribly lifelike characters—the good ones and the bad—in order to learn from them. They were offering us ideals (and nadirs) of behavior by which to guide ourselves, wisdom that might help shed light on the motivations of the people around us, and hope to keep us going. In the same way, Jack and I are offering up our stories about our failures and successes, alongside our thoughts about our favorite novels, so you can learn from them without experiencing quite as much humiliation, agony, and loneliness as we have! We're not here to say: *Do as we have done*—far from it. If anything, we're here to say: *Read. Live. And think. It'll help you to love.*

MUCH
ADO ABOUT
LOVING

Prepping Yourself for Something Real

THE HELL JAR

Why It's Your Problem If No Guy Is Good Enough

ACCORDING TO MAURA

If you'd asked me, back in my early twenties, why I was still a virgin, I would've told you I was holding out for true love, even as I was becoming increasingly concerned I'd never find it. Why? The only guys who ever seemed to really like me were schlubs I wasn't that into, whereas the dudes I yearned for either never gave me the time of day or dated me only long enough to discover, it seemed, that I wasn't who they wanted.

Was there was something deeply wrong with me? Was I cursed? Was there a dark watermark on my soul that those boys could see after they spent enough time with me in broad daylight? For years, I was convinced there was. But I also thought not being sufficiently attractive enough was at least part of the problem, for two reasons. The first was my body, and the second was my face. I was boy-shaped: mostly breastless, mostly waistless, and broad shouldered. My nose seemed disproportionately large, my bottom teeth were incorrigibly crooked, and, as my father liked to inform me, my ears made me look "like a car going down the street with both doors open."

But if you managed to take your eyes off my Dumbo wings for a moment so you could look a bit closer at my romantic history, you

might find that my memory was rather selective. Sure, my grade-school crush John-John had no interest in me and was totally hot for my best friend, Kirsten. But a few subsequent dudes on whom I'd had knee-weakening, trembling-hand crushes *did* end up liking me back. The real problem was that the more into me those guys became, the more unappealing they seemed . . . till finally I couldn't stand them. Casualties of my messed-up heart include a certain Ashton Kutcher lookalike and Doors fan I dated during my junior year at the Academy of the Holy Angels; a glimmering-eyed, wavy-haired, indigo-skinned painter whom I knew during my senior year at Dartmouth; and especially, especially—oh, how it pains me to think of it now—beautiful Dave Bradley, an aspiring sculptor who worked at KULTURAs books in DC around the time I started my first "real" job, with *The Washington Post*'s website. (That tweed hat he always wore, which would've looked affected and idiotic on any other guy, but on him looked sexy and weather-beaten; that manly body that narrowed into a tiny Robert Redford waist; those Popeye forearms that made me lose the power of speech for a good minute or two whenever he lay them down on the table between us—oh, Dave Bradley!)

Ask me now what my problem was back then and I'd finally be able to tell you (thanks to about a billion hours of head-shrinkage). But before I do that, let's talk about a young lady with a similar problem: Esther Greenwood, the heroine of Sylvia Plath's darkly funny and very autobiographical novel *The Bell Jar*. I know some of you are already saying, *Oh, Maura, isn't that book a downer?* I'm happy to tell you it's not—not really. Though the protagonist, Esther, *is* struggling with a serious depression, she's also a comic genius who was having sex in the city long before anyone had ever heard of Carrie Bradshaw or booty texts.

While still in college, Esther lands an internship at an elite women's magazine in New York, where she quickly begins to feel like a fish out of water. What's bothering her isn't just the sense that she doesn't

fit into that world of perky, perfectly coiffed young women. She's also agitated by the cultural pressure to become a wife and mother, two duties that would interfere with her professional ambitions.

Her distaste for marriage seems to stem, in part, from the substandard setups she was constantly subjected to at college. As she puts it: "I hated coming downstairs sweaty-handed and curious every Saturday night and . . . finding some pale, mushroomy fellow with protruding ears or buck teeth." The fungilike men would add insult to injury by dissing her. "Of all the blind dates I'd had that year not one called me up again for a second," Esther complains.

Despite her conflicted feelings and perceived inability to meet members of the opposite sex who *don't* resemble toadstools, Esther does eventually enjoy some success with a male of the species. When she's a junior, she begins dating an attractive young med student—a Yalie named Buddy Willard. She has a crush on him for five years before he starts noticing her, and in the very beginning stages of the courtship, she still adores him. But the more attention he pays to her, the more she finds herself disliking him. (Sound familiar?) And by the time he decides he'd like to marry her, she's decided she hates his guts. He is, she thinks, "an awful hypocrite."

The hating of his guts is sparked by the misbehavior of his penis. Buddy has led Esther to believe that he's a virgin who is uniquely sexually aroused by her. But she's disabused of this notion one night when Buddy suggests they strip naked before confessing to a summer fling he'd had with a waitress from the Cape Cod hotel where he'd been a busboy. "After [hearing] that, something in me just froze up," Esther says. Though Buddy hadn't cheated on Esther, she's outraged that he presented himself in such a false light—and probably pissed, too, that she let herself be fooled. I understand entirely: At least twice in recent memory I've had the experience of believing that a guy is practically head over heels for me only to realize, no, he's actually dating two other women simultaneously. We all want to believe we're

special, that we inspire feelings—sexual or emotional; ideally, both—
that no man has ever had before. But after one too many unpleasant
moments of truth, I've come to realize you can never assume a man
isn't seeing other people till you've discussed the matter with him. In
fact, you'd be better off assuming he *is* dating others—and that he's
no virgin either!—unless he explicitly says otherwise.

Believing herself motivated by nothing more than indignation,
Esther distances herself from Buddy and becomes determined to
lose her virginity to someone else—and soon. After procuring an
intrauterine device, she scans the perimeter to find the perfect male
to initiate her. By "perfect," I don't mean to imply she's looking for
her "other half," or even a guy who looks like a Ken doll. Rather, she
wants someone who is highly intelligent, so she can respect him, and
experienced enough that he will counterbalance her sexual clueless-
ness. Equally important, she wants to do it with absolutely no strings
attached—or, as she puts it, to do it with "somebody I didn't know
and wouldn't go on knowing—a kind of impersonal, priestlike of-
ficial."

Soon enough, during a day in Boston, she meets a young math
professor named Irwin. After coffee, twenty-six-year-old Irwin sug-
gests they go back to his place for a beer. Esther consents, and,
luckily, he turns out to be a halfway decent guy rather than a psycho
killer. The only sword he impales her with is a fleshy one—and they
never see each other again after they do the deed.

That priestlike official description, incidentally, was almost exactly
the description I had in mind when I finally decided it was time to
find a devirginizer . . . at age twenty-eight. I'd been holding out for
true love, so I told myself, but found I had an eight-hundred-pound
gorilla instead: No one ever seemed right—and the longer I waited,
the higher the stakes became. (On top of that, starting around age
twenty-five or so, more and more men seemed to think me freakishly
repressed rather than admirably idealistic whenever I mentioned the

state of my hymen.) I decided that before it got any more difficult, I should break the seal.

So I found someone I liked enough, respected enough, and felt comfortable enough with—but not *so* comfortable that I had any silly ideas about falling in love. A Harvard-educated writer type from LA whom I'd met at a December party in New York, he was smart, funny, kind, kinda hot, and quite quirky. We went on a couple of dates during the week he was in Manhattan, and I explained my virginity problem. Unlike a lot of other men I'd discussed it with, he didn't seem to think my chastity was completely insane; he was also up for being my Valmont. It seemed that I could get deflowered without getting attached.

Still, it took me a while to psych myself up for it. Having waited so long, did I really want to give up now? Did I really want someone I didn't love to go down on my permanent record as the devirginizer? It took me a few months to figure out that the answers to those questions were yes and yes. On the eve of my twenty-eighth birthday, I flew out to California to get things over with. On the big occasion, we did the deed . . . and we did it again and again and again . . . and then I flew away two weeks later. And that was pretty much that between me and Mr. Valmont.

Back to Esther: The way she handles her virginity situation is of a piece with a larger pattern of behavior—a fear of intimacy and commitment—which starts to become clear by the way she reacts to Buddy. Sure, he misled her a bit, but he didn't cheat on her. My guess is that what upset her most wasn't Buddy's sexing it up with the waitress so much as her own strong emotional reaction to the news. Realizing that she could be so upset by Buddy freaked her out deeply; the idea that he could hurt her like that triggered her internal defenses, and she decided to cut things off before any further emotional mayhem could occur. The potential for deep pain implied by any serious relationship fed her fear of marriage in general. But she tells herself

the real reason she doesn't want a husband is because he'd only tie her down. As she puts it, "The last thing I wanted was infinite security . . . I wanted . . . to shoot off in all directions . . . like the colored arrows from a Fourth of July rocket."

A lot of us worry that being in a serious relationship might cause us to stagnate, that it will confine or constrict us in ways that we won't like or might not be good for us. *I* always seem to fret, when I meet a guy who seems like a halfway plausible possibility, that I'll begin to deteriorate intellectually because I won't be able to spend as much time reading and writing, since I'll be spending more of my free hours with him; that I'll become more boring because I'll no longer have new dating adventures; that I'll generally become lazy and complacent.

Admittedly, though, I'm putting the horse before the cart here. Isn't my goal in life not to be smart or interesting so much as *content?* Isn't happiness what I'm really after? And if I find that in a relationship, is it *such* a big deal if it cuts into my private time a little? I suppose what really unnerves me is the idea that I might become emotionally dependent on another person. It's scary when you start to count on someone. Because people's feelings often change—and when they change from love to something less, as happened with Sylvia Plath's real-life husband, the poet Ted Hughes, it can be psychologically disastrous for the person left behind. Hughes started cheating on her when their two children were still babies; after he moved in with his mistress, Plath killed herself. A mere month after *The Bell Jar* was published, she stuck her head in the oven. (Years later, Hughes's mistress killed herself in a bizarrely similar manner.)

What would happen to me if some man became the cornerstone of my life, only to abandon me? What happens if I find the love of my life and he dies—the way the great love of my father's life, my mother, did, after they'd been married barely a decade? Her death, when I was eight years old, debilitated both my father and me so

severely that I've long been wary of getting too closely attached to anyone else. And considering that Plath's father died a couple of weeks after *she* turned eight—almost the exact age that Esther, her fictional double, was when her father passed away—I'm sure Plath's psychology was similar to mine. There's nothing like the agony of a young parent's death to make you swear subconsciously (or maybe even explicitly) that you will never ever again let yourself get that close to someone.

But I've also realized that I need to overcome my fears if I'm ever to have one of the most satisfying and meaningful life experiences around: being in a healthy long-term romantic relationship. I've realized there's truth to the old saying about how it's better to have loved and lost. And I've finally, finally gotten to the point where I've turned about 155 degrees (if not quite 180) from where I used to be. (You'll hear more about all this in the chapter called "Cowards' End.")

So if you're like Esther and me—if you become appalled by any and every guy you've ever had a crush on as soon as he likes you back—please, for your sake, ask yourself what's up with that. Think about why you wouldn't be a member of any two-person club that would have you as a member. Don't tell me that it's only the buck-toothed portobellos who ever like you. Own up to your intimacy issues. Deal with your bad self—and then get serious about finding a good guy.

Jack says:

Maura, I think your final point is a good one: The mushroom guy (assuming he has a little backbone) isn't always bad. My feeling is that both genders put too much investment in looks when they're

picking partners. That's fine for short-term things, but you don't want to narrow the pool too much when you're looking for a long-term partner. I like the strategy of finding a diamond in the rough: a really great guy or gal who appreciates being with you and might not be an obvious looker but—this is crucial—has something about him or her that you find sexy. If he's got hands or eyes or shoulders or something that you can cathect to, that you can use to channel some serious erotic energy, then the fact that the rest of him might not look so great can be less of a problem. Now, if he doesn't end up being able to please you in bed, that's another problem . . .

You're also dead on about the not wanting to be in any club that would have you problem. If that's the way you go about looking for a lover, how could you ever be happy? If that's how you've been operating, either change your ways or get some therapy—fast.

Chapter 2

OVERLY GREAT EXPECTATIONS

Why Idealizing Someone Can Come Back to Bite You

ACCORDING TO MAURA

Oh, great expectations! Those delicious, dangerous thoughts. Our exaggerated fantasies about what might come of a new love affair (or, more insidiously, a long-term obsession) feel so good that we return to them again and again, getting high on the delicious images in our heads. Maybe after a few months of working with a flirtatious co-worker—who nonetheless has never made a legit move—you find yourself imagining what it would be like to cook a candlelit dinner for him, spend the weekend together by the fire at his place, go on a ski vacation with him, spend the holidays with his family, and live happily ever after. Or, following two or three dates with someone who has made it clear he's not over his ex and probably will never be, you're dreaming about what it will be like to move into a penthouse with him, full of dark wood furniture and tulips and books, where you'll have his adorable babies and live happily ever after. Or you've barely kicked off some sexual affair that seems completely untenable but oh-so-enjoyable when you begin fantasizing about running off with a certain someone to small-town Vermont, where you two will run an organic farm, keep cows and chickens and pigs, and live happily ever after.

Plenty of us replay the same daydreams over and over—just about as often as we hit the "refresh" button on our computer screens to see if we've gotten any new emails from the man who plays the leading role in our imagined dramas.

We're like children who can't stop surreptitiously sticking their fingers into the icing—or like crack addicts, going back for one more hit.

Why do I make such negative comparisons? Because I know from experience that our ideas about what might come of an infatuation are all too often dangerous mirages, calling us to them only to throw us pitilessly against their rocks. Vivid as they may seem in our heads, they're often inspired by dizzy delusions rather than real-world evidence that a long-lasting romance might be at hand; we see what we want to see rather than reality because our fantasies are such pleasant distractions from our dissatisfying lives.

Oh, but Maura, what's the big deal? you might be thinking. *Who are we hurting? We all need to escape sometimes, don't we? Would you stop being a killjoy?*

No, lovely readers, I won't. Because the big deal is that when we let ourselves get hung up on guys who are out of our reach, for whatever reason, we waste valuable time, sometimes even years of our lives, betting on people who will never come through for us. And whenever an unlikely fantasy is shown up as a fraud—because, for example, we find out the guy we're obsessed with is dating the chick in marketing—the pain we experience is in direct proportion to how much we've let ourselves fixate on him. So it's in our best interests to keep our great expectations in check; otherwise, the *ignis fatuus* might destroy us.

Now, you might be thinking, *Fair enough—but how in the hell are we supposed to stop ourselves from thinking about SOMEONE WE CAN'T STOP THINKING ABOUT? Answer us that!*

I *will* answer, by way of an outstanding literary example of someone with wildly unrealistic romantic notions: Philip Pirrip, aka Pip,

the protagonist at the heart of Dickens's deeply charming novel, *Great Expectations*. Pip—a young orphan with a sly sense of humor—was raised by his irascible sister and her kindly, illiterate husband in a small English village. Pip's uncle, a blacksmith named Joe, began schooling him in the way of iron-making when he was still a child, but about the time the book opens, Pip starts to think manual labor is beneath him. As he tells a friend, "I am disgusted with my calling and with my life." He yearns for a different existence, one that will take him away from his small town and into the big time.

His latent sense of inferiority was awakened by a fellow orphan— the beautiful, snobby Estella (played by Gwyneth Paltrow in the 1998 movie co-starring Ethan Hawke, which I do not recommend). She is the ward and protégée of the town's wealthy eccentric, old Miss Havisham—one of the most famous characters in all of literature— who became rather deranged after her youthful jilting by a man who defrauded her out of a small fortune. (Talk about great expectations foiled!) Since that moment, Miss Havisham has worn her bridal gown day in and day out. She still has the decaying decades-old wedding cake lying on a table in her mansion, where it has become a "black fungus" overrun by spiders. And, as one of Pip's buddies informs him, she is rearing Estella "'to wreak revenge on all the male sex.'" Despite the fact that Estella treats Pip "as insolently as if [he] were a dog in disgrace," (or maybe in part *because* she does), he develops a serious infatuation with her. Though they have only fleeting encounters, he obsesses about her, imagining how perfect his life would be if she were by his side. Her ongoing condescension seems only to increase Pip's desire for her approval. As he puts it, "I admire her dreadfully, and I want to be a gentleman on her account." If he can somehow escape the poverty he was born into, he thinks, Estella will take him seriously.

That's a big "if"; there seems to be no way to overcome his circumstances. But then he comes of age and learns that an anonymous

patron wants to change his life. Like that—snap!—Pip finds himself
abruptly ushered into a world of money, privilege, advantages, and so-
cial status. He believes he is well on his way to procuring Estella—in
part because he thinks that his secret benefactor is Miss Havisham;
that she's blessed him with his newfound wealth *because* she's grooming
him to become Estella's husband.

Before I tell you more about what happens between him and
Estella, let me say that Pip's is something of a Cinderella story, and
there's a reason that both the folk story and *Great Expectations* (and all
the other stories about disadvantaged kids who find a way out of un-
happy circumstances) resonate so deeply with huge numbers of read-
ers, generation after generation: Many of us feel that we've been born
into the wrong life. Wrong because of cruel parents—or dysfunctional
parents, or absent parents, or simply clueless parents. Wrong because
of poverty. Lack of opportunities. A disappointing genetic inheri-
tance. Who hasn't hoped, at some point, for a fairy godmother or
Prince Charming (or Princess Estella) to lift us out of our suffering
into a gorgeous life?

Yet some of us, like Pip and myself, are more susceptible to run-
away romantic fixations than others. We're the ones tortured by con-
stant anxiety that we're not fancy enough, not well-educated enough,
not attractive enough, not brilliant enough, not rich enough, not suc-
cessful enough—or all of the above. We assuage our pain by convinc-
ing ourselves that an exceptional person—like Estella, for Pip—will
someday recognize something special about us and thereby sweep
away our feelings of inadequacy, discomfort, and alienation, enabling
us to finally feel at home in the world. But it's no coincidence that,
often, the person we fixate on is unattainable in some way—because
he's married, for instance, or simply indifferent. Why do we do that?
Because deep down we think we don't really deserve happiness or
love, so we put ourselves into situations that make obtaining it fairly
impossible.

Dickens knows (as do I) that insecurities as deeply rooted as Pip's (and mine) aren't quickly overcome. As such, his novel doesn't have the kind of happily-ever-after ending that the story of the glass-slipper girl does. (Which is not to say Dickens hasn't written any fairy tales; *Bleak House* is a marvelous one.) No sudden fortune, or blossoming of love, would've alleviated the deep sense of inferiority parentless Pip has lived with from a very young age. Similarly, no amount would magically soften hardheaded Estella.

But slowly, slowly—over the course of many years—Pip admits to himself how miserable he always is around his inamorata; he starts to see how defeating it is to love her as he does—in a way that is "against reason, against promise, against peace, against hope, against happiness." He begins facing up more honestly to his sense of inadequacy rather than hoping to paper over it with money or a marriage. Eventually—after going through some serious personal traumas—he gains a stable sense of self-worth by cultivating his kind side, helping some friends, and reuniting with the father figure he used to be so ashamed of, even though the dear man loved him so well: Joe.

How are *you* supposed to avoid idealizing someone simply after reading this essay about a cautionary tale when it took Pip the better part of a lifetime to realize his mistake? Good question. I wrote this damn essay, and *I* have trouble doing it myself. Just ordering yourself to quit thinking about the person in question won't work. So instead, what I recommend is thinking *more* about the person you've been obsessing over—but in a new way. Imagine you've won him over. Let's say you *are* living together. Will you really be able to do that? Will you feel comfortable? If so, will that, and simply that, permanently render your insecurities moot? Will getting into a much-coveted relationship suddenly cure all that ails your soul? Will having the ideal companion mean that you never again wonder, *Am I good enough?*

If he happens to be *very* stable and *very* in love with you, he *might* help you overcome your anxieties somewhat. Nonetheless, in my experience, low self-esteem doesn't go away overnight, and if you have it, simply getting to a point where you're *willing* to be in a relationship with a loving person takes work (as I touch on in my chapter about *The Bell Jar*). But you don't need anyone's approval or help to begin strengthening yourself psychologically. Simply spend more time doing things you feel proud of—like learning a new language; reading books you've always thought you should read; improving your vocabulary; volunteering; or simply putting some effort into treating the people around you (and yourself, too) with dignity and compassion.

As for how Estella ends up . . . well, I don't want to give too much away. But after many years, she and Pip bump into each other again and she's changed rather dramatically. Her youthful beauty is gone—and yet, after a moment's reflection, Pip decides that "its indescribable majesty and its indescribable charm" remains. As she tells Pip: "[S]uffering has been stronger than all other teaching, and has taught me to understand what your heart used to be. I have been bent and broken, but—I hope—into a better shape. Be as considerate and good to me as you were, and tell me we are friends."

Pip promises her that they are. Do they finally become more than that? I'll say no more except that sometimes I think there is no better love than that of a good pal.

Jack says:

Maura, you ask an important question: How are you supposed to avoid idealizing someone? You're totally right about needing to sort out your feelings about yourself and making sure you feel like you

deserve to be with whomever has caught your eye. I'd also add that you need to recognize how human it is to put on the rose-colored glasses and always take that into account (for two more literary cautionary tales, see the chapters "Bride and Prejudice" and "The Tragic Mountain").

The other thing I would mention is to be aware of how the other person is likely to have on the pink specs at the beginning as well. I'm a disaster early in relationships because I'm always so entranced and hopeful that I end up giving women the idea I really love them well before I do or could. In the early months, take everything with a grain of salt. And remember, a relationship isn't judged by how good the good is; it's how you work through the bad that will make it last for the long haul.

THE HEART IS
A LONELY LITTLE GUY

What to Do with All That Longing

ACCORDING TO JACK

There are times in most people's lives where loneliness can feel like a fundamental human state—you're born into the world alone and you die alone, the saying goes, as if there were no hope of full connection or fundamental sharing. And there are people—I fear I am one—who never stop experiencing the world this way, who, even in the throes of what we all call love, still feel a separation and an itch for something closer.

In my twenties, I wrote a short story called "Three Shades of Longing." It was only minimally autobiographical, but the reality is that my whole life to that point (and perhaps since) has been about that ache—in pretty much every shade. Ever since I was a teen, I just wanted to be a husband and a dad, to have the intimacy and connection of the loving family unit. But to this day the conventional forms of those things have eluded me.

And thus I'm incredibly sympathetic to the needy, the searching, the discontented—all those seeking what Chaucer in his fourteenth-century English called "the dredful joye, that alwey slit so yerne" (i.e., disappears so quickly), one of his definitions of love. Like cracked decanters, some of us can't stay full, and there remains a bit

of faraway sadness behind even the richest joys. A part of me thinks this sadness makes the joys sweeter, just as the fleeting life span of the mayfly makes its struggles and beauty that much more exquisite; it may live but an hour, but it will do so aloft.

Writing, of course is a great refuge for the lovelorn and woebegone (as Henry Miller said, "Words are loneliness"), and of all the Eleanor Rigbys of the literary world, the young Carson McCullers ranks up there with the Brontë sisters as among the most plaintive and most poignant. *The Heart Is a Lonely Hunter* is McCullers's first novel—written when she was twenty-one—and though she married young (at age twenty), the story makes it clear that her life prior to then had been the emotional equivalent of gazing out a prison window.

The novel is a little heavy-handed, a common downfall in the works of precocious youth, as it weaves its message among five plotlines, each centered on a character filled with longing: a deaf-mute, a Marxist would-be revolutionary, a bar owner, an African-American minister, and a young girl (who we can take to be McCullers). The Marxist and the minister long for others to understand their ideas and put their beliefs into practice; the other three, however, reach out with their hearts, hoping for connections that they struggle to find.

When the novel starts, we get what is effectively a parable in the story of Singer, the deaf-mute. He befriends another deaf man and comes to love him and speak to him endlessly in sign language, despite the latter seeming neither to understand nor even to care. As the novel progresses, person after person will come to speak to Singer— each thinking that Singer's tolerant silence means he understands them perfectly, despite the fact that he doesn't speak back.

What's sad—and telling—is how willing each of the characters is to believe that someone finally gets them. None, not even Singer, realize that they're projecting understanding onto their interlocutors, but in reality each remains alone.

This one-way, no-return language and the illusion that it's actually dialogue will be familiar to any of you who have loved in vain. We sustain ourselves with optimism that our feelings are coming across, but eventually the person says or does something that makes us realize they don't love us back and that our words and actions were for naught.

That shipwrecked feeling of putting note after note into bottle after bottle, wondering if any will reach its destination, clearly afflicted each of the protagonists of *The Heart Is a Lonely Hunter*. The Marxist tries to rouse the masses but his exhortations go unheard; the preacher struggles for Afro-American unity and dignity but can't even get his own family to understand; the young girl, Mick, tries to talk to the other children about her love of music (even Mozart) and tries to build herself a violin that of course doesn't play. She sums up her life, thinking "how lonesome a person could be in a crowded house."

Although Mick is the stand-in for McCullers herself, the most poignant character is the deaf-mute Singer, whose deaf friend ultimately moves away, leaving him without anyone he could even think would understand what he's saying. But that doesn't take away the longing, the desire to speak, even if a part of him knew that he wasn't being comprehended. McCullers describes how: "[H]is hands were a torment to him. They would not rest. They twitched in his sleep, and sometimes he awoke to find them shaping the words in his dreams in his face . . . Then sometimes when he was alone and his thoughts were with his friend, his hands would begin to shape the words before he knew about it. Then when he realized, he was like a man caught talking to himself . . . and he doubled his hands and put them behind him. But they would not let him rest."

Maybe I'm just maudlin or overfull of undershared love, but I think my heart and spirit itch that way, too, to speak out and share and connect, not to stay quiet when they have so much to say.

I named this chapter "What to Do with All That Loneliness," and

I suspect that by now you think that neither Carson McCullers nor I would have an answer. And yet I actually think she did, even at the tender age of twenty-one.

The secret lies in Biff, the bar owner and widower, who keeps his bar open deep into the night. "He would never close up for the night—not as long as he stayed in the business. Night was the time. There were those he would never have seen otherwise. A few came regularly several times a week. Others had come into the place only once, had drunk a Coca-Cola and never returned."

He is a kindred spirit to the older waiter in Hemingway's famous short story "A Clean, Well-Lighted Place," who says: "I am one of those who like to stay late at the café. . . . With all those who do not want to go to bed. With all those who need a light for the night . . . I am reluctant to close up because there may be some one who needs the café."

There are other people who share the longing; they wander and seek, just like us.

So the answer must be for us to be like Biff: to keep the bar open, to keep a candle in the window, never knowing who might stop by. Who knows, maybe they'll need us as much as we need them.

Chapter 4

BRIDE AND PREJUDICE

*Does Wanting to Get Married
Give You Champagne Goggles?*

ACCORDING TO JACK

I'm willing to go down on record saying that *Pride and Prejudice*, though one of the finer novels in English literature, can actually sometimes be among the most damaging for female readers. Consider the setup: The smartest and most selective of five sisters (Lizzy) meets a dashing but exceptionally arrogant, inconsiderate man (Darcy) who has nothing but disdain for her family and social group. She responds by being cheeky with him—which seems appropriate—and later when he decides he has a crush on her and proposes, she rejects him. But then, in the remaining chapters of the book, Lizzy slowly realizes that all her misgivings about him were false, that really he's rather dreamy, and that, yes, she loves him back and pines for him to propose again.

What?

Okay, I know any Austen fan would say that Darcy was misunderstood and Lizzy's correct by the end in thinking that he's a great guy. Don't worry, I get it; the title refers to each of the protagonists' respective failings: Darcy's pride, which supposedly he gets over, and Lizzy's prejudice, her tendency to "willfully misunderstand" people, as Darcy at one point accuses her of.

And fine, let's say that's all true. But even if Austen isn't leading us down the primrose path and the plotline should be taken at face value, I'm still concerned about the subtle messages the novel sends. Seriously, think about it. Until she gets deeper insight into his character (and even then I'm dubious), what exactly, other than Darcy's looks and bad-boy diffidence, would make Lizzy change her initial estimation, much less fall for him completely? Are there some Brad Pitt abs we haven't heard about? Doubtful.

No, instead it seems that it's the fact that he pays her "the compliment of such a man's affection"—and by "such a man" she means such a condescending, judgmental tool. But being a jerk to everyone except one singled-out person is a strategy assholic men use all the time to make women feel "special." Maybe I'm acting the older brother here, but if Lizzy were in my family, I would say that anyone who behaves like a prick the first few times you meet him probably *is* a prick, and just because he decides to give you special treatment later, you shouldn't fall for it. The minute it's no longer to his advantage to play you favors, he's likely to go back to his crappy default behavior.

That's one reason why *Pride and Prejudice* is so potentially damaging to women readers: It sends the subtle message not to dismiss arrogant SOBs out of hand and also that if you're the one they finally show favor to, you should give them the benefit of the doubt. Know how that plays out in reality? Read our chapters on "The Brief Wondrous Life of My Last Relationship" or "Moby Dickheads" for examples: You'll probably end up getting cheated on, mistreated, or underappreciated. If a man starts out giving you a bad impression, you should probably keep believing that impression until he gives you *plenty* of firsthand proof that he's really changed. And guess what? That change isn't likely.

And that's not all. Even granting that the conventional wisdom about *Pride and Prejudice* is spot-on—namely, that the prejudice in the

title was Lizzy's *before* she fell for Darcy—I actually think she might be as prejudiced or more so *after* he proposes to her, as if thinking about marrying him clouds her senses to what she understood about him earlier. And what's especially surprising about that is that Lizzy, of all the significant female characters in the book, starts out the least desirous to get hitched. While her friend Charlotte was so obsessed with the idea of getting wed that she accepted the hand of the ultra-dull Mr. Collins, Lizzy clearly values her own wit and identity enormously—and gives them full reign, even if they threaten her husband prospects.

That's why, if you have a hard time believing the complete transformation of Darcy (and we'll examine that in a second), it's very hard to understand why Lizzy would actually come to believe that she loved him. So, to explain, at least in part, I'd like to introduce the concept of "champagne goggles": A distant cousin to the distorting beer goggles you get from too many Heinekens at the pub, champagne goggles come with the natural human desire to get married, causing us to romanticize, idealize, or otherwise let off the hook potential partners and their various flaws. Champagne glasses create the opposite effect that being overly picky does; they let people slide by when they should be held accountable, and they keep us from asking questions that really are vital—especially if you're about to try to spend the rest of your life with someone.

Some of us want so badly to get married that we don't notice that we're settling, don't see that we've sacrificed not only our romantic notions but also our core values, just so we don't have to risk ending up alone. Neither Maura nor I have gotten married yet, but I've seen the majority of my friends marry. When I ask myself, How many of those marriages would I want to be in? The answer is, not many. Too often it seemed that people rushed into things a little too quickly—maybe out of great expectations, but maybe just out of fear.

In the world of *Pride and Prejudice*, I will admit that of all the champagne goggles, Lizzy's might be the least distorting. (Charlotte's were far worse, as were Lizzy's father and mother's, and her sister Lydia's, among others.) But even her example serves as a kind of cautionary tale. So let's look at the evidence up close and see if you really think she had adequate grounds to fall for Darcy, or if, at least a little, she too fell under the romantic spell and gave him a bit too much benefit of the doubt.

The fact that Darcy starts out the book as a d-bag goes pretty much without question. He is brought from London as a guest to the provincial ball attended by Lizzy and her sisters, and when his friend Bingley says he must dance, Darcy responds: "I shall certainly not. Your sisters are engaged, and there is not another woman in the room whom it would not be a punishment to stand up with." Then, when Bingley suggests he dance with Lizzy, Darcy "looked for a moment at Elizabeth, till, catching her eye, he withdrew his own, and coldly said, 'She is tolerable, but not handsome enough to tempt *me*; and I am in no humor at present to give consequence to young ladies who are slighted by other men. You had better return to your partner and enjoy her smiles, for you are wasting your time with me.'" Damn, Holmes!

And before you think I'm jumping to conclusions, the italicized "me" in the quote above isn't my doing; it's Austen's. So how are we supposed to think this guy is anything other than what the various attendees of the ball conclude about him by the end of the evening: the "proudest, most disagreeable man in the world"?

So, yes, that's the pride of the title, and from that we're supposed to think that Austen has baited a trap for us, leading us to conclude that Darcy really is a bad person, only to turn the tables later (and, yes, by the end she does a *lot* of explaining). But what if she baited it too well; when a guy really seems that self-centered, should a woman as smart as Lizzy *ever* fall for him?

As the book unfolds, two things are in play: 1) Darcy apparently turning out to be something other than what Lizzy thought; and 2) Lizzy feeling guilt about having misjudged him (if in fact she did). The first of two big turning points comes when she discovers that Darcy didn't ruin his sister Georgiana's engagement with a guy named Wickham (Darcy actually saved her from it, because Wickham turns out to be a scoundrel). She realizes that all along Wickham had been lying and Darcy had been aboveboard, and suddenly she laments, "How despicably have I acted! . . . I, who have prided myself on my discernment! . . . Had I been in love, I could not have been more wretchedly blind." Well, don't worry, honey; from my vantage, you're about to make up for it by being equally blinded *by* love!

Still, she isn't quite smitten. But later, after his character is attested to by his old housekeeper, and he acts less conceitedly in front of Lizzy and her relatives, she decides that maybe his pride is really his only flaw and that's not so bad.

Here is the critical paragraph:

The respect created by the conviction of his valuable qualities, though at first unwillingly admitted . . . was now heightened into somewhat of a friendlier nature by the testimony so highly in his favor . . . But above all, above respect and esteem, there was a motive within her of good-will which could not be overlooked. It was gratitude—gratitude, not merely for having once loved her, but for loving her still well enough to forgive all the petulance and acrimony of her manner in rejecting him, and all the unjust accusations accompanying her rejection . . . Such a change in a man of so much pride excited not only astonishment but gratitude—for to love, ardent love, it must be attributed . . . She respected, she esteemed, she was grateful to him; she felt a real interest in his welfare; and she only wanted to know how far she wished that welfare to depend upon herself, and how far it would be for the happiness of both that she should employ the power, which her fancy told her she still possessed, of bringing on the renewal of his addresses.

In a nutshell, for him to forgive her for spurning and misunderstanding him, he must *really* care for her (thus the ardent love line), and therefore, Austen (and Lizzy) concludes, she should be really grateful and try to make him happy.

Yuck! That's not a reason to marry someone! Sure, some of Lizzy's reasons for saying no to Darcy's proposal were in error, but there were others that are legitimate (the fact that he steered Bingley away from her sister for no good reason, his lack of emotional intelligence, etc.), and does she really have proof that those have gone away? Sure, he's not conceited with his friends (and, by the end, he makes an effort with Lizzy's family as well), but what about everyone else?

Nor does it end there, because once she decides that she might want to marry him, she can go ahead and use the rose-colored flutes to idealize him to her heart's content. After Wickham runs off with one of Lizzy's sisters (the youngest, Lydia) and Darcy intervenes to help, our heroine gushes to herself: "He was as generous, she doubted not, as the most generous of his sex . . . he was exactly the man who, in disposition and talents, would most suit her. His understanding and temper, though unlike her own, would have answered all her wishes." Uh, I hate to say it, ladies, but giving away a little money when you're rich is no big deal (and the real award for the "most generous of his sex" should probably go to the kind-to-everyone Bingley).

It's not that Darcy is a bad guy; Lizzy clearly could have done much worse. It's just that I think she falls for him way before she really should.

The critical moment for me comes very late in the book when Darcy admits that he had been a pretentious boob his whole life until Lizzy showed him the error of his ways. Okay, at that point even I can forgive him the misdeeds of earlier. But by that point, Lizzy has already accepted his proposal! To me, that should have been the

point where she started to think to herself that maybe he'd be a good enough guy for her. Yes, call me a grouch, call me *un*romantic, but I think a lot of readers are swayed by their own romantic notions (and the exceptionally well-acted screen adaptations of Darcy) to realize how dangerous a man like that would be in real life, or how out of character Lizzy was in swooning so soon.

Of course she and Darcy do end up getting married, and apparently they live happily ever after, but that's literature for you. In real life, however, one wants to be a little more circumspect and a lot more careful. Just as beer goggles in a bar can send you home with someone you're *really* not psyched to wake up next to, when we want too much for a relationship to work, and especially when we want to get married as much as Jane Austen characters seem to, there's far too great a chance of putting on the champagne goggles and not taking them off until it's way too late. So do yourself a favor: Don't give up on your original prejudices too easily until you really have proof.

No matter how many kisses, sometimes a frog is just a frog.

Maura says:

Jack has a good point: Even though there's much less pressure now than there was in Jane Austen's day, plenty of women still feel like life won't be complete unless they marry. And I know how over-powering the fear of spending life alone can be, particularly after all your college chums have married off, one by one, and you seem to be the only single person left standing in all of Facebook, the United States, Earth, the Universe, Infinity. But you're not. And don't forget that any marriage will come with opportunity costs; in the years that I've remained solo, I've made some of the best friends of my life, whom I might never have gotten close to if I'd been someone's

spouse. What's more, the dizzying divorce rate—50 percent of all first marriages come to an end—should serve as a reminder that rushing into "I do" could mean you soon find yourself saying, "What have I done?" Getting hitched isn't a guaranteed path to bliss, especially if you're female. In fact, researchers have found that unhappy marriages not only increase women's risk of depression and feelings of stress; bad unions also up their odds of becoming diabetic and developing heart disease. A ball and chain *and* hypertension? Who needs it?

That said, my money is on Lizzy and Darcy living happily ever after. *Sense and Sensibility* (which I discuss in chapter 15) made me a reluctant Jane Austen fan; *Pride and Prejudice* made me a die-hard Darcy champion. Sure, the guy's an oaf around most women. But given the choice, I'd take an awkward man (who is kind to his employees and closest friends) over a king of charisma like Wickham any day of the week, and twice on Sunday. Fun as it is to meet charmers at parties, dating them can be painful. They so much get off on sweet-talking new people that after a while, you can begin to feel like you should never turn your back—and to wonder how many seductions go beyond mere words. When you pair off with a Darcy, you can rest easy. Instead of carrying on with half the English countryside (or a significant portion of the American hinterland), he'll save his charms for you.

LIGHTBULB IN AUGUST

How to Have a Clue When He's Just Not That Into You

ACCORDING TO MAURA

Though *Light in August* was published in 1932—more than seventy years before the release of a certain bestselling self-help manual for daters—it's hard to read Faulkner's mesmerizing classic without having the urge to say to one of the main characters, "Yo, chick, don't you get it? He's just not that into you!"

The young lady in question is Lena Grove, a pregnant (or "swole-bellied") country girl from Alabama who's been traveling for four weeks in an almost idiotically confident search for the feckless young drifter who impregnated her, Lucas Burch. He clearly never had any intention of attaching strings: He and Lena didn't do much more than have sex, from the sounds of things, and they didn't even do *that* more than a dozen times—and whenever they did, Lucas would sneak through Lena's bedroom window after dark to get with her. (That way he escaped the notice of her older brother, who'd become Lena's guardian following their parents' death when she was twelve.) Louche Lucas, in other words, wasn't exactly wining and dining her. And when she tells him she's pregnant, he's horrified. But he's also enough of a bullshit artist that he's able to immediately set the stage for weaseling out of his responsibility. Telling her he feels like he

should find a way to make more money, so he can take better care of her and their unborn child, he asks her: Doesn't she think he should leave town to find a new job? And send for her once he gets settled in his new situation?

Lena, buying his hogwash, agrees that it's a good plan. So when silver-tongued Lucas hightails it out of town, effectively abandoning her and their child, he goes with her blessing.

Lena, Lena, I bet you're saying, *have you no clue, girl?* I was. But even while I thought she was a complete nincompoop, I felt for her. After all, who among us hasn't believed what she's wanted to believe, rather than the obvious truth, when it comes to a guy who has made sweet love to us, unleashing all that oxytocin and other bonding hormones?

As the months pass without a word from Lucas, Lena's pregnancy begins to show. Her bro, sensitive guy that he is, calls her a whore and accuses the right man, but Lena continues to defend Lucas and to stubbornly insist that he has nothing but the best of intentions. She is, as Faulkner puts it, "unshakable, sheeplike, . . . [with] that reserve of patient and steadfast fidelity upon which the Lucas Burches depend and trust." Pathetically, she has so much faith in Lucas that when she's more than seven months along, after learning of a rumor that he works at a lumber mill in Jefferson, Mississippi, she begins hitching rides in that direction—convinced that the reason she hasn't heard from him yet is because he's just lost track of time! Never for a second does she doubt that he'll be anything but overjoyed to see her once she tracks him down.

Everyone Lena encounters catches on pretty quickly that Lucas is a scalawag and that she's kind of an idiot. But they also pity her, almost begrudgingly—and out of a sense of Christian duty, they help her as she continues on her journey. When one Good Samaritan tries to hint that maybe, just maybe, this Lucas person is not exactly the salt of the earth, Lena defends him with "calm unreason," saying, "[H]is plans just never worked out for him to send for me in time,

like he aimed. Going away among strangers like that, a young fellow needs time to get settled down. He never knowed [*sic*] that . . . he would need more time . . . than he figured on. Especially a young fellow full of life like Lucas, that likes folks and jollifying."

Lucas has bent Lena out of shape somewhat literally—and she bends herself out of shape trying to make excuses for him. She does what so many modern women do: In flagrant violation of Occam's Razor, she ignores the most obvious (and least desirable) explanation for a man's bad behavior—that he would be perfectly happy if he never saw her again and is going to great lengths to avoid taking any responsibility for what he's done. Instead, she believes what she wants to believe. She goes to great geographical lengths—from Alabama to Mississippi, to be exact—to find him, because it's so difficult for her to even consider that Lucas doesn't care about her the way she presumes he does.

There's a long and rich literary history of women being in denial when it comes to the charismatic roués in their lives. But just because there's a tradition of it doesn't mean we ladies should simply give in to our reality-denying instincts. Rather, we should pay more attention to our feelings when any kind of treatment makes us feel dissatisfied or miserable—and when it does, we shouldn't twist ourselves into knots concocting explanations for the men who let us down. If an hombre seems to be blowing you off, don't do him the favor of making up an excuse about why his behavior *isn't* as inconsiderate, disappointing, inappropriate, or as downright rude as it appears to be. Do *yourself* the favor instead, and ask him politely and calmly why he didn't call when he said he would, or why it took him nearly a week to respond to an email, or why he got the number of some other girl as you were standing right next to him at a holiday party once. (Remember that, Andrew Stern?) Similarly, remember that men are not, simply by virtue of gender, completely clueless—much as we'd like to believe differently. Though there is some wiggle room if the specimen

in question is young, once a dude reaches his middle or late twenties, chances are that if his behavior is inconclusive or lukewarm, he probably isn't feeling it. One of my male friends, a very successful lawyer in his thirties, puts it this way: "While a guy may be too swamped at work to write the long, thoughtful emails some women seem to expect, he's never too busy to follow up in some way after a good date—even if only by sending a quick text at four a.m. as he takes a car home from the office."

Does that mean if you don't hear from a date within twenty-four hours of your first rendezvous, all is lost? Not necessarily, but consider toning down your hopes accordingly. And it's fine to give him the opportunity to explain himself once or twice after instances of flaky behavior—but if there's a third time, tell him that he has struck out. Have standards. Don't just play hard to get; *be* hard to get. Whatever month it is—August, January, April, you name it—screw in that lightbulb and force yourself to accept the cold hard facts: You, as a human being, are entitled to fair and reasonable treatment, and if he can't see that, there's no reason you should be blind to it, too.

AS YOU'D LIKE IT (OR SO YOU THINK)

The Mistakes We Often Make

JANE ERRED

Why It's Silly to Put Principles Over Passion

ACCORDING TO MAURA

If Jane Eyre were a real person, alive today, I get the feeling I'd like her. I could almost see myself trying to befriend her. She has a strong sense of personal morality; she's smart, resilient, resolute; she's a good storyteller. And yet . . . I bet I'd get annoyed with ol' Jane a lot of the time, because she can also be forehead-smackingly priggish. She's so concerned with doing the *proper* thing that she often does the *wrong* thing—or at least she does it big time at the most dramatic point in the novel that bears her name. By adhering rigidly to principle rather than letting herself be guided by common sense, Jane makes a crucial error in judgment on her wedding day. In order to stick to the letter of Christian law, she commits a terrible act of self-destruction: She decides to sever all ties with the man who had been her fiancé—the love of her life—after some disconcerting news about him is revealed. As a result of her breaking off the engagement, they both go into severe emotional tailspins and do crazy things that nearly kill them; one ends up disfigured as a result.

Before I tell you any more about Jane—before I discuss why she *should* have run off with her guy, even though he had a pretty big strike

against him—let's talk about friends of mine who cast aside custom (as Jane should have) in favor of happiness.

One of my best buddies from college—Jo—was a raven-haired, cleft-chinned beauty, a city girl who dressed in old corduroys and men's sweaters and wore a big chunk of turquoise on one finger. During our sophomore year, she met a charismatic quarterback, a golden Midwestern boy with eyes like sea glass who loved indie rock and bong hits—Rick. Something very close to love at first sight ignited. The more they got to know each other, the more the flames were fanned. Within a few weeks, they were inseparable: clearly head-over-heels for each other, and blissfully giddy.

After they'd been together about six months, Jo told me and a few other close friends a big secret: She and Rick were planning to elope. Nope, no bun in the oven. They were just certain they wanted to spend the rest of their lives together and wanted to make the whole thing official—but suspected their parents wouldn't be thrilled. As it turned out, just about all of Jo's buddies weren't either. They said, "But you're so young! You have your whole life ahead of you! Get more experience before you jump into anything!"

My take on it was different: Jo seemed happier than I'd ever imagined she could be. I'd been worried about how hard she pushed herself socially and scholastically—regularly staying up all night so she could make the party *and* write the paper, chain-smoking all the way through. But with Rick looking out for her, she started taking better care of herself—or *he* did—and suddenly all you had to do was look at her to see how happy she was. I figured that even if the marriage dissolved a few years down the road, the experience would be great for her.

In the face of so much disapproval, I wouldn't have been surprised if even Jo had her doubts—but luckily, the faith that she and Rick had in each other ran deep. Undeterred by the nervous Nellies, they tied the knot on the rugby field, surrounded by about two dozen

cheering coeds and three golden retrievers. Now—many many years later—they're still married, with four (four!) of the most beautiful kids I've ever seen. He's thriving professionally; she has a law degree and does philanthropic work. After bucking tradition to follow their hearts, they're still just about the most lovey-dovey couple I know.

Like many of the naysayers who tried to caution Jo and Rick, Jane Eyre has a wrongheadedly conservative attitude about her own marriage. That's particularly aggravating coming from her, because she's otherwise a pretty independent thinker, willing to question the status quo and able to see hypocrisy when it's staring her in the face. After being orphaned as a baby, young Jane is raised by a cruel aunt who mistreats her at every opportunity, belittles her relentlessly, and looks the other way when her son physically terrorizes his poor cousin. Jane eventually speaks truth to power, telling her aunt: "I will never come to see you when I am grown up, and if anyone asks me . . . I will say the very thought of you makes me sick, and that you treated me with miserable cruelty. . . . You think I have no feelings, and that I can do without one bit of love or kindness, but I cannot . . . you have no pity."

Offended by her insolence, Jane's aunt sends her off to a boarding school for impoverished girls. Lowood Institution is pretty rough for a while, too: A nasty clergyman who heads the school subjects the girl to severe privations (even refusing to allow one girl her gorgeous curly hair!) and the malnourishment they experience as a result seems to effect a typhus epidemic. That leads to an investigation—and the sadistic headmaster gets replaced. Soon enough, Jane finds a contentment at Lowood that she has never known before; she spends eight years there—six as a student and two as a teacher. But eventually, feeling it's time to move on, she takes a position as the governess for the ward of a wealthy loner named Rochester. Rochester comes off as a curmudgeonly bachelor at first, but Jane quickly begins to feel he is a kindred spirit. Though it seems he's about to get married to

a flighty young social butterfly, a sense of comfort and camaraderie develops between him and Jane that neither thought they would ever find in another person. Before long, she develops deep feelings for her pensive employer—and in kind, he shows himself to be pretty much monomaniacally devoted to her. The love between them is about as pure as it gets, in life or literature. She thinks, "I feel akin to him—I understand the language of his countenance and movements . . . every good, true, vigorous feeling I have gathers impulsively round him." He says that he will be "ever tender and true" to Jane, with her "clear eye and eloquent tongue, . . . [a] soul made of fire, and . . . [a] character that bends but does not break—at once supple and stable, tractable and consistent."

When he surprises plain Jane—whose homeliness is mentioned again and again in the novel—by proposing they get hitched, she is pleased from bonnet to boots. She accepts. But during their marriage ceremony—right at the moment when the minister invites anyone who knows of a reason why the couple should not be joined in holy matrimony to speak then or forever hold his peace—a stranger steps forward to accuse Rochester of being *already married*, to a wife he hasn't divorced . . . !

Dun, dun!

Plot twist!

Say it ain't so, Ro'!

But as it turns out, poor Rochester *does* have a wife—a lunatic named Bertha who has completely lost her mind, to the point where she often behaves like a wild animal. When Rochester takes Jane to see the woman, she thinks, "What it was, whether beast or human being, one could not, at first sight tell." (Charlotte Brontë, the author, was criticized, at the time, for her harsh description—and I will admit that Bertha's "craziness" is so extreme that it's a little hard to believe.) After Jane and Rochester leave Bertha to her caretaker, he explains how he ended up married to such a disturbed individual.

When he was a young man, his wife, a great beauty and heir to a good fortune, seemed perfectly sane. But her rich relatives could see that the girl would succumb to the same disease that had destroyed her mother. (Some scholars think Brontë was describing schizophrenia.) So they and Rochester's own conniving family tricked him into marrying her, though he never loved her. Her mental problems grew at a dizzying rate till she was barely functional . . . at which point Rochester tried to get a divorce, only to discover it was legally impossible. His wife swiftly became his albatross. For years, he has kept her in a hidden room in his manor house, where she is watched over round the clock. To add to Rochester's miseries, his wacko spouse seems touched with evil: One time, while her nurse was in a drunken sleep, the crazy lady escaped and nearly killed Rochester by setting fire to his bed.

Hoping to take his mind off Bertha, he spent many years traveling around the world, trying to find solace in mistresses, to no avail; the women he met either didn't interest him, or wanted him only for his money. He returned home to England in "a hard, bitter frame of mind," as he puts it; "corroded with disappointment," without much faith in humanity, but especially down on women. "I began to regard the notion of an intellectual, faithful, loving woman as a mere dream," he says. A mere dream . . . *until* he met Jane, that is.

Upon finally revealing his life's story to her, Rochester adds, "After a youth and manhood passed in unutterable misery and half in dreary solitude, I have [found] for the first time what I can truly love . . . my better self—my good angel." He importunes Jane to move to the south of France with him, to a "white-washed villa on the shores of the Mediterranean," where they can live *as if* they are married—and he emphasizes that he will both call her his wife and think of her as such, legalities be damned.

But Jane is too pigheaded to do that; though she's sympathetic to Rochester's plight, she recalcitrantly refuses his offer, because her religion forbids such a thing. She's such a puritan that she can't look

past the fact that while Rochester may be legally married, his wife is completely out of touch with reality . . . to the point that she can no longer communicate by way of human speech. When Jane tells Rochester she can't so much as *hang out* with him anymore, let alone shack up with him, he says, "Then you condemn me to live wretched, and to die accursed?" And Jane prudishly replies: "I advise you to live sinless. . . ."

Lame, Jane.

That night, reflecting on whether or not refusing Rochester was the right decision, she thinks:

> *I will hold to the principles received by me when I was sane, and not mad [with love]—as I am now. Laws and principles are not for the time when there is no temptation; they are for moments as this, when body and soul rise in mutiny against their rigor. . . . If at my individual convenience I might break them, what would be their worth?*

Shortly thereafter, she tells herself again that she acted correctly: "Yes; I feel now that I was right when I adhered to principle and law, and scorned and crushed the insane promptings of a frenzied moment."

Weak reasoning, if you ask me. Rather than questioning whether or not the law she's being guided by was conceived to apply to someone in a position like hers, she falls into line all too quickly. Ralph Waldo Emerson might have told her that being foolishly consistent is "the hobgoblin of little minds." Contrary to what Jane seems to think, we don't have principles in order to transform a morally gray situation into a clear-cut black-and-white scenario. Principles are mainly cognitive shortcuts that help guide us through our daily lives, shaping our behavior, informing our decisions, and enabling us to make choices quickly. In the vast majority of cases we don't think much about whether or not it's okay to marry a married man, because we *know* it isn't, and we have the laws to prove it. And yet, on very rare

occasions, there's nothing more *right* than running off to the south of France with someone who can't get legally divorced.

Not that I'm advocating adultery—hell, no. But sometimes we have preconceived notions about the kinds of people we should *never* date; maybe it's someone we report to at work, or someone who lives in another state or country, or someone of a certain age, or someone who is a Republican or a Democrat, or someone who works at a butcher shop even though we're vegans. Most of the time, these categories probably *do* help us not to waste our time with people we'd never be terribly compatible with . . . except in the cases where someone who falls into our "Never" category makes us happier than we ever imagined possible.

If you ask me, Jane had a very primal belief that she didn't deserve what she so deeply wanted—in large part because she suffered so much abuse and neglect during her childhood, and in small part because she's conscious that she's not attractive. So I think *part* of the reason why she didn't fight for her love is because she was convinced, on some level, that she wasn't meant to have it.

I'll conclude with this suggestion: When and if you're lucky enough to find true love, don't muck it up with mindless adherence to convention. Throw away that list of requirements. Maybe you never thought you could spend the rest of your life with a guy who's divorced or has kids or has an ex who is foaming at the mouth—but if he makes you feel more blissful than you ever imagined possible, please go for it.

And if someone invites you to live in his whitewashed villa on the shores of the Mediterranean? I'm pretty sure you don't even need to be in love to do that. But you do need to invite me to visit.

Chapter 7

THE TRAGIC MOUNTAIN

Beware of Leaping Before You Look

ACCORDING TO JACK

Who has not seen, fluttered, wondered, wished, implored, and lost, all in the brief viewing of the unknown face in a train window, the passing of the stranger on the street, at someone in front of you in a lecture, or imagining the life of a lone reader in the corner of the café? But instead of acting on our impulses, we play them out in our imagination. We sit silently, wanting a windfall but doing nothing, like a farmer facing foreclosure who stands in the middle of his field with no shovel in hand and simply looks up.

It is a uniquely human gift to see reality for something that it isn't, to take the life in front of us and perceive it instead into a shape we want it to be. But how partial are these imaginings, how incomplete? Our love affair with the solitary reader is created only to the point of embrace or undress; her morning surliness, our socks left on the floor—these aren't part of the idealized picture we trick ourselves into thinking has been painted in full.

Proust famously fantasized about farm girls he saw from the train (and, yes, he meant boys), but he also notes how much of their beauty was a function of seeing them from afar, when he was unconsciously Photoshopping in the details. Our desires are so much easier to

project when not thwarted by too many intrusions of truth, allowing the mind to fabricate what the heart covets and the heart then to say, "Yes, it might be so." Over time and given more exposure, our hearts do their best to keep their prized sugarplums dancing by falsifying or misconstruing the empirical records as much as necessary. Perhaps the brain from some distant sequestered place attempts to sound the alarm of self-deception, but do we always listen? Clearly we don't want to hear. It is a painful thing to wake from a pleasant dream, the music fled, as Keats would say, and what lover among us wouldn't dream, dream, and go on dreaming?

I, for one, often wear the rose-colored glasses far too long, seeing my lovers as I need them to be instead of as they are (and need themselves to be). For me, the moon of honey can hang in the sky it seems for years on end, its light like pollen dappling down, distorting and intoxicating. People like me are often called romantics, often called fools, and of course we are both, unwilling to give up our soul's dearest hope for transcendence. If we're lucky, we eventually mature and discover how to extract rapture from reality; if not, we're doomed to disappointment, forever seeing life as a fraction of what our imagination would have it be, lost in longings that we will never realize.

Literature is strewn with such cautionary tales of romantic daydreamers, some appealing and sympathetic in their persistent search for more—like Anna Karenina—others almost despicable in their unwillingness to take life as it is—like Emma Bovary. In one of my favorite novels, however, Thomas Mann's *The Magic Mountain*, we see one of the most elaborate and subtle investigations of infatuation, projection, longing, and romanticism that literature has to provide.

The bearer of the infatuation is Hans Castorp, protagonist of *The Magic Mountain*, and its object is Clavdia Chauchat (my favorite name in literature, even if her last name borders a little too obviously on the French *chat chaud*—hot cat!). Madame Chauchat—yes, she is married when Hans meets her—is a patient at the tuberculosis sanatorium in

the Alps (thus the magic mountain title) where Hans has gone to visit his cousin—and to which he is rather quickly admitted for apparent illness of his own. (This is one of the things I love about *The Magic Mountain:* its deft rendering of illness as a kaleidoscopic metaphor for an astonishingly varied range of elements of the human condition.)

Madame Chauchat is also afflicted, but to Hans she is marked, above all, by being utterly "heedless." She arrives late to the dining room each evening, allowing the glass door behind her to slam (and though at first Hans considers this a sign of ill breeding, eventually the sound becomes a Pavlovian trigger for his desires!). The heedless Clavdia Chauchat is languid in her motions, otiose in temperament, indifferent in affect, and untoned in body. And yet Hans is obsessed. She is marked by broad cheekbones (later called "hyperborean") and epicanthic "Kirghiz" eyes (meaning she looks Caucasus Far Eastern). He is intrigued; he continues to try to make eye contact from across the room (they all have accustomed seating from which they do not deviate), yet she is too heedless to notice—or is she?

It's the perfect setup for a young man's infatuation, and finally Hans finds himself dreaming of her coming to him in the dining room and putting her hand, palm up, for him to kiss. "And at that there swept over him anew, from head to foot, the feeling of reckless sweetness." And from that, young Hans Castorp soon believes himself in love: "He needed only to think of Madame Chauchat—and he did think of her—and lo, he felt within himself the emotion proper to the heart beats."

In my paraphrase of Hans's enamoring, it is true I'm condensing a number of meals, perhaps dozens of jarrings of the verandah glass, but the important element is that he reaches this communion with his own heart *without her ever acknowledging him!* Mann observes that "when a man is in Hans Castorp's state—or the state he was beginning to be in—he longs, above all, to have her of whom he dreams aware that he dreams." But despite all Hans's maneuverings to make eye contact in

the dining room, Clavdia Chauchat never looks his way. And are we even surprised? Might that be in part why he "loves" her? And so it goes, the imagining, the projection, the fantasy, the arousal, until at last their eyes do meet, wordlessly, and Hans concludes that her look speaks to him in the familiar of a friend, not the formal of a mere acquaintance. But of course he does not know, nor do we, given how willing we humans are to interpret in our own favor. She is married, sickly, Russian, and perhaps over thirty; what would she want in our phthisic young hero?

Of course, the flip-side exergue of trumped-up infatuation is a similarly trumped-up jealousy, and Hans is not immune. As it turns out, the director of the sanatorium has also fallen under Madame Chauchat's spell, and when Hans learns first that he is painting her portrait and then that he is going to x-ray her—to see her very insides (X-rays were brand new when the novel was written in 1924), Hans is devastated at these varying degrees of access to and intimacy with her.

Later he sees the portrait—a "rather botched performance"—and yet it is she. The director explains: "Yes, there's something about her—if you get the detail right, you botch the ensemble. Riddle of the sphinx." Riddle of the sphinx, perhaps, but it is clearly the riddle of roseate glasses: how to see and not see, to take in an object as it is yet not alter it as you want it to be. The painter, too, is smitten; there is something he wants to see in the painting, to harness and portray on the canvas. But the thing he seeks is unlikely to be Clavdia Chauchat.

For Hans, there does come a crescendo, a fateful private encounter with his dream girl—and on, of all times, Walpurgisnacht (a German free-for-all, sort of half Carnival, half Halloween). Drunk on champagne, and because they are in costume, she allows him to speak to her in the familiar. They flirt, and eventually she tells him she is leaving the next day for another sanatorium that might help her more.

Hans, for his part, finally says—and on his knees no less—that he is only at the sanatorium because his love for her is the source of his illness, that he loved her the moment he saw her and even before he saw her, and that he was brought to the magic mountain drawn by the love he had always had and always would have for her.

Did I say he was a little delusional?

Mature woman that she is, she calls him her "Carnival Prince," puts a paper hat back on his head, says he knows how to flatter a woman (in the German way), and tells him he'd better go to bed because his fever will be up. The next day, Hans receives a keepsake— the X-ray image of her internal self that he so coveted—but Clavdia has left.

When she eventually returns, she has brought a lover. Lost in the "kingly man's" shadow, little Hans sees that his crush is hopeless and eventually goes down the mountain to become a soldier. His love affair comes to an end, dissipated like the smoke he never knew it was.

It is fitting, and it's a warning—one I know I myself must heed. For some of us, the seeds and soil of love can exist entirely in our minds; we nurture them, they flourish, but whatever blooms they yield are false, and time will prove them so. Just as old-time traders would bite a coin to test its metal, we romantics need at times to be suspicious of our feelings and confirm that they're genuinely what we hope them to be.

Rose-colored glasses can be nice to wear, but reality, of course, is often not as we would have it. Every love relationship deserves to be given a fighting chance—and for that to happen, it has to take root in reality, not fantasy. If we never ground our feelings and assure their truth, we risk one day waking up next to the person we thought we loved, suddenly wondering who they are.

BRIGHT NIGHTS, BIG SHITTY HANGOVERS

The Perils of Drinking and Hooking Up

ACCORDING TO MAURA

Plenty of people spend copious amounts of time going out to bars and clubs in the hopes of meeting a potential mate, and it's no mystery as to why: Large numbers of people congregate at those types of places, and plenty are lonely; the ready availability of alcohol helps to grease the social wheels. So, sure, that may not be a bad method for *meeting* someone. But is it any way to start a relationship? Doubtful. Not least because it can be quite difficult to gauge the alcoholic distance between relaxing enough to flirt with the attractive person sitting on that barstool next to you, and relaxing *so* much that you do things you regret the next day. (Things like, oh, I don't know . . . going home with a guy who is *not* Mike, the bandmate of your saxophonist friend, as you thought, but someone you cannot remember having ever seen before.) What's more, you may have very different hopes than whomever you brush up against that night; you may be looking for love, whereas he may be looking for nothing more—and sometimes nothing less—than a one-night stand.

But don't take my word for it. Instead, listen to the never-named narrator of Jay McInerney's excellent and autobiographical debut

novel, *Bright Lights, Big City*—a book written in the second person, as if it were one long direct address. The book begins while the narrator—let's call him Mr. Bright Lights—is in the midst of a nocturnal Manhattan adventure with Tad Allagash, a wealthy, prep-school, banker type who is also a high-flying social kingpin. Though the boys' evening started with champagne on the tony Upper East Side, when we meet them, they've spent the last four hours in a somewhat unsavory nightclub that might be called Heartbreak; Bright Lights can't remember. The time "has already turned on that imperceptible pivot where two a.m. changes to six a.m." as it has a tendency to do during our misspent youths. While doing his best to blow off some girl who is yammering on about how the club "used to be a good place before the assholes discovered it," Bright Lights surveys the scene, thinking: "[F]or some reason you think you are going to meet the kind of girl who is not the kind of girl who would be at a place like this at this time of the morning. When you meet her you are going to tell her that what you really want is a house in the country with a garden."

In other words, guys—and girls—often categorize any member of the opposite sex whom they meet at a nightspot as someone they can't take seriously, particularly if it's after a certain hour. As another novelist, Kate Christensen, puts it in her book *In the Drink,* a "bantering dive-bar pickup" usually leads to "drunken sex, a rushed exchange of phone numbers afterwards on a subway platform, then other nights with more dive-bar bantering and drunken sex." What it usually does *not* lead to is a thriving, happy relationship.

If I had to do a very rough approximation, I'd guess that the ratio of trips made to bars in the hopes of meeting someone to get serious with compared to the number of times that actually happens must be something like 520 to 0. Or, at least, I myself made about 520 trips to bars over the course of my twenties. (There are 520 weeks in a decade, and I think it's not hyperbolizing to say I visited an average of at least one bar per week during that period.) I *met* quite a number

of guys. I kissed plenty of them on dance floors, smoked joints in the back with a few, did a little more than that with some others. But did I ever come across my next boyfriend? Ha!

Getting trashed *will* help you find your way into some deeply uncomfortable situations. Like the one I got into with a guy named Guy, whom I met at a bar on the Lower East Side one night when I was out with a bunch of friends. A few of us decided to continue drinking back at my place; I made the mistake of inviting Guy along. He ended up spending the night (as did two friends who crashed on my pull-out couch). We didn't do much but kiss—I may have also hiccupped a few times—before I passed out. The next morning was uncomfortable: I was hungover, and though Guy was hot, in a Crispin Glover kind of way, he was also a bit strange, in a Crispin Glover kind of way—whispery and awkward. Explaining that I felt physically ill, I asked him to leave. As I closed the door after him, I hoped that was the last I'd see of him. That night, however, he called and left a message. I ignored it. He called the following night and left another message. And again the next. . . . Four nights and four unreturned voicemails later, someone was screaming my name from the sidewalk beneath my apartment. I peeked out my bathroom window. Yep: Guy. I tiptoed into my closet, terrified, and hid there for about ten minutes, until he gave up.

When he called a few minutes later, I dealt with it: I told him he was freaking me out and asked him to please leave me alone.

"But you acted like you liked me so much!" he complained.

"I was totally wasted!" I protested. "I had no idea what I was doing!"

It took me an hour to convince him there would never be anything more between us. But much as I was annoyed, I also felt for him. I myself had also, more than once, developed wild fantasies after a late-night snog-fest with a reprobate, only to have my hopes dashed in the bright light of day.

So, yes: Barhopping can help you find someone who is inter-ested—*too* interested. It can also help you find a jerk or two. Like that guy I mentioned before, who was *not* Mike, friend of the saxophon-ist, but, rather, someone I'd never met before. After a long night at a jazz club in New York, I was so drunk that I didn't even realize I was in my apartment with a complete stranger—the non-Mike—until I came to as he was poised above me, unwrapping a condom. "What the hell are you doing?" I said. Luckily, he left pretty quickly when I said there was no way I'd sleep with him. Considering the condition I was in, I had to wonder if the guy was also into doing it with corpses.

Though I can't speak for that paraphiliac, my guess is that he hadn't been hoping to find *love* before leaving his apartment that evening. I think it's also fair to say that during the unfortunately long period of time when I was spending every weekend getting very wasted, *I* certainly wasn't ready for a relationship, though I thought I wanted one.

Bright Lights isn't ready either. What he's looking for as he stands there gaping at the other inhabitants of Manhattan's underworld—what he's been looking for during his hard-partying tenure as Al-lagash's side kick—is a mind eraser (and I don't mean a drink with Kahlua with vodka and tonic). His wife, a model named Amanda, left him months earlier, and since then he's spent plenty of long nights pinballing through Manhattan, hoping to find some "earthly salva-tion" in the form of a woman, though he knows what he's more likely to find is "the sexual equivalent of fast food."

After getting fired from his job, Bright Lights hits a new low and finally admits to the reader (and, thanks to the second-person voice he's using, to himself) that the pain of his mother's recent death is tearing him apart. He'd married Amanda, despite serious doubts, dur-ing his mother's struggle with cancer in the hopes that his wife might help him get through the imminent loss. But she only made things much worse by dumping him shortly after the funeral.

With this big epiphany under his belt, Bright Lights realizes it's time for him to change. He tells himself, "You will have to go slowly. You will have to learn everything all over again." He's ready to be the guy he wants to be: "the kind . . . who wakes up early on Sunday morning and steps out to cop the *Times* and croissants. Who might take a cue from the Arts and Leisure section and decide to check out an exhibition. . . . The kind of guy who calls up the woman he met at a publishing party Friday night, the party he did not get sloppy drunk at."

The kind of guy who doesn't meet chicks at bars. The kind of guy who knows if you go to a place that might be called Heartbreak, you probably won't find much more there than that.

LOVE IN THE TIME OF ONLINE DATING

Why Too Much Emailing Can Be Dangerous

ACCORDING TO MAURA

Years ago, shortly after I moved to New York, I got whipped into a romantic frenzy over a man I didn't really know, thanks mainly to an extensive email exchange we had. Oh, he could give good prose! But as much as the voice that he wrote with aroused me, I had no idea if his lips would make me start speaking in tongues, seeing visions, or experiencing nirvana: Two months in, we'd never met. We'd started corresponding through an online dating service while I was doing a journalism fellowship in Europe. He seemed to be a genius; brilliant lines effortlessly burst forth from his fingertips like spit from theater actors in moments of high dudgeon. When he mentioned he was working on a book, I was sure it would be the next Great American Novel; I'd never met a man who was as impressive "on a sentence level"—as the graduates of creative writing programs like to say—as he was. And then there were his pictures: I kid you not that he looked like a blond version of Superman—like young Christopher Reeve if he'd been born with hair like white gold. And when I googled him, discovering recent pictures of him at different New York parties, he looked in real life just like he did on the dating site—how refreshing!

During my stint abroad, an intense virtual intimacy developed

between us. And though I didn't go as far as *telling* Mr. Great American Superhero I was in love with him, I thought I might be—particularly on the day when I couldn't find the friend I was supposed to meet up with in Prague, and he talked me through the minor crisis via email. Twenty years older than I, he was wise in the ways of the world; he had all sorts of smart insights about things like traveling, solitude, and the literary world. He became psychologically embedded in my brain; whenever I was having a distressing moment, I'd think of him and perk up.

As my summer came to an end, I flew home—and I'd barely hailed a cab at JFK before Superhero and I rendezvoused at some swank bar. My heart skipped a beat when I walked in and saw him sitting at a little table in the corner. But as I got closer, I was gripped not so much by nerves as . . . alarm. With perhaps a touch of repulsion. My stomach began churning out ice cubes. He looked almost exactly as I'd expected—*except* he seemed to have been put into one of those computer programs that add two decades to your image. There was a progression of semicircular wrinkles under his eyes, rippling down like pond waves made by a stone. His skin might have been drawn by van Gogh, for all the fine red crosshatchings in it. His hair wasn't blond so much as a silvery yellow. He looked so old!

Whereas the age difference had seemed cool to me before, I suddenly thought: *Pedophile!*

I'd sort of dated one older guy before that—a bad-boy restaurateur who was in his forties; he co-owned a few well-known spots in the city. But his dark hair hadn't gone gray, he was in great shape, he was playful; long story short, he didn't look or seem very old. (Or maybe he did and I was just having too much fun making out with him in the back of his hired Rolls to notice.) But that night in the bar, I was a girl in my early twenties realizing that I wasn't that into older men—as I sat staring at one with whom I'd been flirting for eight weeks.

I tried to be as polite as possible as we drank from our fishbowls of red wine. But my feelings were so at odds with certain sentiments I'd typed to him while the Atlantic separated us that I felt slightly ill. When he said something about spending the night holed up in each other's arms, I may have physically recoiled. Excusing myself due to exhaustion, I said good-bye . . . and that was the last time we saw each other.

Something similar happens in one of the most decadently readable love stories around, *Love in the Time of Cholera*. In it, a young telegraph office employee by the name of Florentino Ariza falls for a snotty hottie named Fermina Daza. For Florentino, it's lightning at first sighting: After delivering a telegram to Fermina's father, Florentino passes by the window where she is sitting; she looks up to see who the visitor is; and "that casual glance was the beginning of a cataclysm of love."

Unfortunately, however, Florentino doesn't have much of an opportunity to win her over. Fermina's mother has died and her strict father keeps her away from boys—especially lower-class *chicos* like Florentino, the bastard son of a single mother. Regardless, Florentino follows Fermina (usually accompanied by her guardian aunt) around town obsessively, hoping to get a glimpse whenever he might. His indefatigable attention inevitably causes *her* to become equally preoccupied with him, to the point where her blood regularly "frothed with the need to [spot] him." Eventually, they begin sending feverish secret letters back and forth. Over the course of two years, though they pretty much never set eyes on each other, they stay in constant contact through their pens—until the wicked mother superior at Fermina's school intercepts one of their notes. When she tells Fermina's hot-headed father about the epistolary affair, he asks Florentino to stop pursuing his daughter—and indicates he'll kill him if he doesn't.

"Shoot me," Florentino responds. "There is no greater glory than to die for love."

Which causes Fermina's father to realize he's up against one seriously love-crazed kid. "Son of a bitch!" he says.

Rather than become a murderer, Mr. Daza takes his daughter away on a year-long journey into the mountains. But even that doesn't stop Florentino and Fermina: With help from telegraph workers in the region, they surreptitiously continue their correspondence.

Eventually, clueless Mr. Daza decides it's safe enough for him and Fermina to head home; she returns "taller than when she had left, more polished and intense, her beauty purified by the restraint of maturity." Soon after they arrive, Fermina notices Florentino in the marketplace. As always, he's wearing the one suit he owns: a black one that used to belong to his dead father, which his mother had altered to fit him. He looks like he has throughout most of his life: "very thin, . . . hair plastered down with scented pomade and eyeglasses for myopia, which added to his forlorn appearance." His feverish love for Fermina has given him the pallor of a sick man—so much so that his mother worried, for a time, that he had cholera. It's Fermina's first good look at him in years—and . . . "instead of the commotion of love, she felt the abyss of disenchantment. In an instant the magnitude of her own mistake was revealed to her, and she asked herself, appalled, how she could have nurtured such a chimera in her heart for so long and with so much ferocity."

When I read that, I wanted to scream *No, Fermina! How could you do that to poor, crazy, adorable Florentino!* Because *I'd* fallen for him—what a wonderful besotted puppy he was, with such a poetic heart! And yet, of course, I also knew how Fermina felt. Being forced to confront an idealized love object in real life can make the heart grow cold. Important as it is to feel connected by an exchange of words and ideas, a romantic relationship is also physical—and often the hopes we build up about a person when we correspond with him from a distance clash with the amount of carnal attraction we feel when we finally come face to face. So Fermina Daza may not have been freaking out about

Florentino's appearance in itself as much as about the great discrepancy between her idea of him, and the reality of him.

Given all this, please do yourself a favor and keep the emailing, texting, and phone chats to a minimum during the early stages of a courtship. Rely on electronic devices primarily to make plans and touch base; put most of your time and energy into face-to-face communications. My rule of thumb, when Internet dating, is to ask a guy to have a phone conversation after we've exchanged ten short emails (five on either side). Most of the time I can tell within a few minutes of chitchatting if I'd like to meet him. But even—and especially—if the talk is going well, my goal is to get off the horn after thirty minutes; the more time spent talking, the bigger the danger of getting overly excited. Similarly, I try to discourage excessive emailing or texting following a first date, even if it's gone exceptionally well, because it can be *such* a time suck—and the only thing truly worth discussing electronically, until you're dating steadily, is when you'll hang out again.

Whatever you do, don't fall into a pattern, as Fermina and I did, of relying on a fantasy for emotional sustenance. That's an excellent recipe for a mental state so illin' that someone might think you have the plague. But it's not a great way to kick off a meaningful romance.

TRAGICOMEDY OF ERRORS

OF ERRORS

Types to Watch Out For

NOT-SO-GREAT GATSBY

Is It Flattering or Creepy When a Guy Persists?

ACCORDING TO MAURA

At first blush, having the love of someone like the fictional character Jay Gatsby sounds pretty wonderful. For starters, he's a hunk, played in the movie by my man Robert Redford. He is so taken by the girlfriend of his youth that he spends years and years transforming himself into a powerful businessman in the hopes of winning her back, after her high-society family disapproves of him. (This, despite the fact that he dated her for no more than a month, *and* she forfeited her promise to wait for him until he returned from the war.) When he learns she's become the wife of a Chicago socialite, he's undaunted: He continues to build his fortune—albeit by shady means, very likely including bootlegging—and combs the Chicago gossip papers for years, hoping to glimpse her name. (This was back in the era B.F.— Before Facebook.) After discovering she's living with her husband in a wealthy community on the Long Island Sound, he buys an enormous mansion on the other side of the bay simply to be close to her. Twice a month, he opens his home up for exquisite parties that feature a full orchestra, a "bar with a real brass rail," and a corps of caterers who make "salads of harlequin designs and pastry pigs and turkeys bewitched to a dark gold." Just about every fancy pants in Manhattan

attends Gatsby's bashes . . . but the only guest he really wants to attract is her.

It sounds pretty romantic—until you think about it a little harder. Wouldn't any guy who's that determined and persistent come off as creepy in the real world? A little pathetic? It's one thing to bump into an old flame, realize the passion you felt long ago is still there, and rekindle things quickly; another for someone to be so infatuated with you that his dogged pursuit determines the course of his life. How could you, or anyone else, ever live up to whatever idealized notion a guy like that has in his head? Isn't it wildly unreasonable for someone to think that a girl he knew so briefly, before she'd really developed into an adult, could be his one and only route to true happiness? Even if he's not an outright stalker, that doesn't mean the situation would work out.

Let us consider the example of a certain Gatsby manqué, a friend of mine named Jason. An incredibly intelligent and very good-looking but melancholy man now in his early thirties, he has, for the last several years, carried a torch for a chick called Dee he dated while they attended creative writing grad school together. Jason seems to believe that success—in the form of literary-bestseller fame—will help him lure her back. Though he's had plenty of romantic opportunities, I get the feeling he thinks all other chicks simply help to distract him from *the* woman, his idée fixe. Jason is so convinced that Dee is the only one for him that he can't take anyone else seriously—never mind that she has been living with her boyfriend for many years.

Why is he so hung up? My diagnosis: He's trying to hold on to his lost youth. He's living in denial so that he doesn't have to face the painful reality that the period when he first knew Dee—when he was newly enrolled in a prestigious fiction program, winning all sorts of writing contests, and thinking (with reason) that he had a brilliant career ahead of him—is irretrievably gone. By refusing to give up on Dee, he assuages the pain related to the other things that haven't

quite worked out the way he wanted them to. (Jason hasn't yet published a book.) By remaining focused on reuniting with Dee—something that still seems within reach—he defers reality. Perhaps Gatsby, too, thinks that winning Daisy back will help restore some of the innocence he lost by fighting in the war and becoming a man of criminal business.

Now, of course, Jason and Gatsby are different in one crucial way: Gatsby has more money than God, Bill Gates, and Warren Buffett combined. But I worry that Jason is setting himself up for tragedy, like Gatsby did. Both want certain impossible things of their Daisy's—things that Gatsby's closest friend, Nick Carraway, sheds light on when he says: "[Gatsby] talked a lot about the past, and I gathered that he wanted to recover something, some idea of himself perhaps, that had gone into loving Daisy. His life had been confused and disordered since then." Gatsby, like Jason, bets that getting back together with his lost love will imbue his life with the meaning and happiness that has eluded him for so long. Like Dee for Jason, Daisy is more—and less—than a person to Gatsby; she's his Holy Grail. She's a guiding light, like the green one at the end of her dock that Gatsby is fond of looking at from across the water. And he is a man who isn't really *anyone*; he has changed his name and fabricated parts of his life story, and no one seems to know exactly what he does for a living. Pursuing her is his identity more than anything else.

Part of Gatsby's problem was that Daisy and her husband were "careless people [who] . . . smashed up things and creatures and then retreated back into their money or their vast carelessness, or whatever it was that kept them together, and let other people clean up the mess they had made." But Gatsby's fanatical pursuit of Daisy was so self-destructive—he completely annihilated his old identity and replaced it with a new one to win her—that it was bound to fail, in one way or the other. As Nick explains: "[T]here were times when even Daisy tumbled short of his dreams—not through her own fault,

but because of the colossal vitality of his illusion. It had gone beyond her, beyond everything. He had thrown himself into it with a creative passion, adding to it all the time, decking it out with every bright feather that drifted his way. No amount of fire or freshness can challenge what a man will store up in his ghostly heart."

Right. Someone like that is a Pygmalion taken with the beautiful creation in his head more than with a living and breathing human. And quintessentially Gatsby-esque though the pursuit of a man like that may be, it's not so great.

Jack says:

Maura, my real question is whether the novel itself is that great (in my opinion, it's okay, just not especially impressive). Yes, that's beside the point, but I do think, especially as the technology of surveillance grows and grows, that obsessive types are riskier than ever. Who knows which of your stuffed animals he's bugging or putting a camera in, hoping to catch you with the pool guy?

That said, there is one kind of near-obsessive guy who gets a bad rap: the boyfriend who's simply just devoted as hell to you but comes off a little like a wet blanket. I know it seems kind of emasculating when a guy likes you *that* much, but isn't that better than one who doesn't like you enough? And is it really somehow disempowering to really, really love someone? I don't think so (and I've been that guy before, I confess), so maybe we need to rethink this one a bit. To my eye, calling an extra good boyfriend a wet blanket is a minor variation on the not-wanting-to-be-in-the-club-that-would-have-you complex. You'd be well served to change your mind on that one.

INFINITE GESTICULATING

Why Do Men Talk So Much?

ACCORDING TO JACK

I've heard it many times: "I can't believe my blind date last night—no questions, just an endless monologue. I couldn't get a word in edgewise. It was like I wasn't even there—except to be an audience."

Want to take a guess as to the gender of the date who wouldn't shut up? And how about the one who didn't get a chance to say anything? Uh-huh. You know it as well as I do.

But why *do* men talk so much, and why do women put up with it? Obviously, it's mostly about cultural conditioning and the way the ego plays out differently, much of the time, for American men and women. For a deeper understanding, though, I thought we'd turn to one of the more prolix, or should I say loquacious, euphuistic, logorrheic, or just plain wordy novels in recent memory: David Foster Wallace's one thousand plus–page, long-talking, synonym-accumulating, reader-taxing, and very, very male (but also pretty incredible) novel *Infinite Jest*.

Reading *Infinite Jest* is a little like being locked in a white unfurnished room—for about two or three weeks—with the smartest (and funniest) professor you ever met, only that professor clearly just whooshed an eight ball or two of fine Columbian up his nose and

is apparently both in a dangerous psychotic state and acute septal pain. It is an absolute babble-fest, going on and on and on, inscribing (predominately) in its large compass the topics of competitive tennis, drug addiction, and contemplated suicide (the author did actually kill himself in 2008).

But what it's about perhaps more than anything is loneliness, the kind of personal and spiritual abjection that would lead one to substances in the first place, then make it hard to kick them, then come in like an absolute mo-fo once you're truly addicted and try to get the monkey off your back. And the way it compensates is through verbiage, as if someone continuing to talk would send the demons back from whence they came, when really each word probably just issues more forth to haunt and harass.

When the novel begins, we find out that its principal character is a seventeen-year-old tennis prodigy who also happens to have a perfect photographic memory and is memorizing the entire *Oxford English Dictionary* (uh-huh). The author then spends the next thousand pages attempting to use as many of the *OED*'s words as he can (as well as a few hundred from *Stedman's Medical Dictionary*). Clearly, we have a bit of a problem.

And in reality, what we have is something that happens in literature more often than people realize: an author acting through his book almost exactly as he would act on a first date—and for the same reasons. He's lonely, insecure, nervous, jumpy, and a little spazzy, in dire need of affirmation, but proud of certain parts of himself and desperate to show those to you (his date).

So he talks. And talks. And talks.

The same thing does not occur, curiously, with women authors. Of the top ten longest novels in English, only one was written by a woman—*Atlas Shrugged*, by Ayn Rand—and I wonder, as heartless as she seems, whether she should even count as a woman.

No, the unhalting tongue—both in books and on dates—is

typically a guy's problem, and thus I find it amusing in *Infinite Jest* how David Foster Wallace makes even his female characters exhaustive (and exhausting) in their descriptions of things.

At one point, the femme fatale (in a quite literal sense in the novel's plot), Joelle, is explaining to Don Gately, the recovering drug addict/house burglar (and one of the few not especially verbal characters), why people would join the so-called Union of the Hideously and Improbably Deformed (UHID). Five paragraphs in, she's still at it, saying:

> *What you do is you hide your deep need to hide, and you do this out of the need to appear to other people as if you have the strength not to care how you appear to others. You stick your hideous face right in there into the wine-tasting crowd's visual meatgrinder, you smile so wide it hurts and put out your hand and are extra gregarious and outgoing and exert yourself to appear totally unaware of the facial struggles of people who are trying not to wince or stare or give away the fact that they can see that you're hideously, improbably deformed. You feign acceptance of your deformity. You take your desire to hide and conceal it under a mask of acceptance.*

Nor does she stop there!

Gately's response is pretty much what the reader has been begging of the author since the novel started: "Use less words."

But, no, DFW isn't going to use fewer (as proper usage would have it) words; instead he'll keep at his utterly desperate attempt to impress you with his lexicon, his knowledge of math and medicine, his verbal alacrity, and his stamina.

The thing you need to understand if you're on a date with a guy like this—or, if you decided to brave it and actually entered in a relationship with such a boy—is that there are endless gesticulators who are aware of and deep down feel guilty and embarrassed by what they are doing, and there are those who have no idea whatsoever. The latter

group, let's call them sociopathic soliloquists, should be avoided at all cost. Their egomania has no cracks; you should get out of Dodge as soon as possible, as you will never matter to them as much as the sound of their own voice.

I don't think DFW is in that camp, though. Gately's response above is a wink to the reader, letting us know that he—the author—knows he's going on too long, as he does again later in his descriptions of the films Joelle acts in. The narrator describes them as appearing to have: "no emotional movement toward an audience . . . Joelle thought them more like a very smart person conversing with himself."

And of course that's what DFW (and a lot of cerebral guys) often do—but also what the good ones fear the most. It's loneliness they want to break out of, but they're so habituated to having no one to talk to (on their level), that they never learn how to make conversational bridges with the rest of us.

It's a double bind, and we should both pity them and hold them accountable. While they really should learn to socialize, learn to self-edit, learn to ask questions and really listen, in many cases they simply can't.

So if you find yourself on the other side of a candlelit table with someone who won't shut up, stop him midsentence. Ask him directly if he's interested in knowing anything about *you*. If he pulls back and apologizes—maybe even confesses that his nervousness got the best of him—then you know the guy might well be okay. If he gets offended, well, he probably didn't want anything but an audience for his ego's long monologue. Check please!

FAREWELL TO CHARMS

The Macho Man—Can He Have a Soft Side?

ACCORDING TO JACK

Back in 2009 when Maura told me she was having a little fling with a fireman, it made perfect sense: firemen are studly—and, since 9/11, clearly the hottest male commodity in New York.

Her announcement came just as I was in the process of finishing a reread of Hemingway's *A Farewell to Arms*, so even I had bohunk dudes on the mind. And you have to understand: For the longest time, this was the sorest of sore topics for me. I grew up the skinniest and weakest kid at school, and since I couldn't even do a push-up, I was positive I'd never be able to get married because I'd never be able to carry a woman over the threshold. And though I eventually realized you don't need to be able to pick up a woman to marry her, it wasn't until my thirties when I decided to add some semblance of muscle to my pencil-pusher's pencil torso. Trust me, though, the scars are still there . . .

But having gotten over my scrawny duckling phase, I'm still in the process of learning how important machismo really is. It's hard to tell sometimes if my body and "masculinity" (what there is of it) are adding to the equation or if women just like me for my book collection (yes, I'm joking). But Maura—I *know* she likes bookish guys—so

I decided to ask her exactly what it was about her fireman that made her choose him for the fling, and really, what it is about macho guys that women in general like so much. I understand the jawline, the confidence, and the tool belt, but apparently there's more to it. This is what she told me:

Macho guys make me feel especially feminine, without even really trying, by doing things like picking me up as easily as they would a laundry bag. It's the appeal of feeling physically protected. And macho guys are usually pretty emotionally uncomplicated, which might be the best part of all.

The strength part I buy, but seriously, Maura, that last bit? There I'm not so sure. Is *anyone* ever emotionally uncomplicated, and, if they were, would that be a good thing? Doesn't emotionally uncomplicated in a man normally mean emotionally unavailable or out of touch?

Well, for this question, Hemingway himself is in some ways the perfect case study. If you read his novels and short stories carefully, you'll see that he had an enormously sensitive heart, though both he and his characters spend a lot of time trying to hide it.

In fact, there might be no writer in history who tried harder than Hemingway to be macho. He spent his life hunting big game in Africa, going to bullfights in Spain, volunteering to drive ambulances for the Italian army, drinking and smoking and gallivanting until he finally took a shotgun to his own forehead at the age of sixty-one. And his characters, when confronted with feelings, tend to back away, clam up, and do everything possible to keep from having to reveal their inner selves.

Hemingway populates his books and short stories with underapologetic men's men (apart from F. Scott Fitzgerald, who asks him if his penis was small in *A Moveable Feast!*), and it's long been noted that Hemingway's writing style itself was an attempt at a kind of prose masculinity, avoiding the unnecessary and getting down to

immediate business. Machismo is clearly a major issue for Papa; in my last book I allude to Hemingway being the author of the novel *Men Without Women* and wondered if that's how he would have liked it, not to have to desire them, not to have to talk after the sex was over or the liquor bottle ran dry.

In his famous short story "The Snows of Kilimanjaro," Hemingway depicts a man dying of gangrene, attended by his wealthy lover and waiting for a rescue plane that won't come in time. (Hemingway himself had gotten very ill in Africa with an intestinal condition, but his plane *did* arrive.) The man, thinking back on his life, realizes that he's spent his days taking women's love, their money, but that invariably he quarreled with them, "loved too much, demanded too much, [and] wore it all out." He finally calls love "a dunghill" and himself "the cock that gets on it to crow." Ouch. Still, despite how poorly the dying man treats his partner, you get the sense that his frustration at dying before he could accomplish what he wanted to do (write the perfect story) got the best of whatever he might have felt for the woman. No one would deny that Hemingway's men are egoists; the real question is whether they can love anyone else.

For the best evidence, I think you have to turn to the novel *A Farewell to Arms*. It's Hemingway's most tender, nuanced portrait of a man's conflicted romantic feelings, and thus most informative on the interaction between men and women.

The plot centers on Frederic Henry, an American serving as an ambulance driver for Italy in World War I who has an affair with a Scottish army nurse, Catherine Barkley. Most of the time in his romance with Catherine, Frederic stays guarded: "Have you ever loved anyone?" she asks him. "No," he replies. Then later she says, "You are sweet." And he replies, "No, I'm not." And finally, when she presses him, saying, "You did say you loved me, didn't you?" his answer is damning: " 'Yes,' I lied. I had not said it before . . . I knew I did not love Catherine Barkley nor had any idea of loving her. This was a

game, like bridge, in which you said things instead of playing cards."

Sure that's what he says, but my theory is that that's the way Frederic wants to feel; he wants to be able to deny that he loves Catherine, but deep down he (and we) suspect he does. Take this very uncharacteristic Hemingway line (Frederic is the speaker):

> *I loved to take her hair down and she sat on the bed and kept very still, except suddenly she would dip down to kiss me while I was doing it, and I would take out the pins and lay them on the sheet and it would be loose and I would watch her while she kept very still and then take out the last two pins and it would all come down and she would drop her head and we would both be inside of it, and it was the feeling of inside a tent or behind a falls.*

When you read that, it's hard to believe that Frederic isn't just afraid of his feelings and doing everything he can to resist them.

To my eye, his relationship to Catherine is similar to the affair late in Cormac McCarthy's *Suttree* (one of my all-time favorite novels): It's one of the few times these ultramasculine writers take women and relationships seriously, allowing real sentiment to sneak through their characters, but then quickly closing the gate behind.

Which leads us to the issue of macho guys in general. The sad fact, in my opinion, is that guys get trained to want to act tougher than they are, or at least to think that toughness and sensitivity are somehow at odds. Yes, many of the most sensitive writers of all time were stupendous wussies (Proust and Henry James perhaps above all), but it's a fallacy to think that having feelings and being studly are mutually exclusive. (I was really surprised, for example, to know that Andre Dubus III, before writing the incredibly poignant novel *House of Sand and Fog* was working as a carpenter and looked like a lumberjack centerfold from *Playgirl.*)

What Hemingway at times makes clear—and to me, these are his *best* times—is that even the toughest guys can run deep, even the guys

who don't want to have feelings can still have feelings, and that doesn't take away from their masculinity at all.

Now, as a kind of pathetic skinny boy, I'd rather macho men *not* get in touch with their inner selves, and of course I'd rather women continue to think that they need to turn to bookish writer-types to get emotional depth (when what they really get is often just narcissism).

But from the other side, when I think about raising sons (and how I was raised), I'd argue that no matter how wimpy and cerebral a boy might be, his parents shouldn't lose track of the role of the body—physicality, strength, confidence, assertiveness (if matched with attentiveness)—all as part of what can be good about being a man.

My mom got this right when I was a teenager when she told me: "There's nothing sexy about a man with no spine."

Of course, machismo is still icing on the cupcake of date-ability. The most important things are still a good heart, the ability (and desire) to communicate, attentiveness and compassion, and a genuine want to be with another person. Those qualities might be rare in macho guys—let's face it, they can be rare in *all* guys—and maybe macho guys are more likely to think they shouldn't possess or show them. But they can, and when you find a guy who's hard on the outside and soft on the in, then you've got a catch.

A REAL PAIN IN
THE AENEAS

Sometimes It's Really Not You—It's Him

ACCORDING TO MAURA

Not long ago, during a uniquely delusional moment, I thought I'd met Mr. Maura Kelly—despite the fact that he'd indicated before we met, while we were still just a couple of strangers exchanging email messages, that he wasn't up for anything serious. I thought I wasn't really either. But then girl met boy, boy was outrageously awe-inspiring, boy seemed smitten with girl, girl starts imagining the babies they'll have together—even though she doesn't want babies! . . . and then boy abruptly bowed out.

When things went so wrong, after seeming (for a brief moment) so right, I thought no other woman in the history of the *world* had ever been as stupid as I'd been. The flags were not just red; they practically had "Go Away!" written on them. In Mr. MK's very first note, he'd said that he was "hoping to meet a smart woman to take out from time to time"—which is very different from "hoping to meet the person I will grow old with." Plus, the kid was nearly ten years my junior, which automatically made the chances of us going the distance much lower. *And* he was finishing up his second year of law school; not exactly the type with a lot of time to get to know a person who was living an hour's subway ride south. But I have a weakness

for younger men and he was *so* exceptionally smart and literary—
he'd quoted Auden during our first phone conversation and gently
corrected me when I'd flubbed an allusion to ancient playwright
Terence—that I couldn't help myself.

After our first date I knew, in my gut, that developing a crush
on this kid was not the smartest idea. But I figured, *What do I have
to lose?* (Just a few months of emotional stability, that's all!) Before
we were four weeks into it, I knew there were all sorts of addi-
tional things that would make it tough, if not impossible, for us
to get serious—not just the huge age difference. He was planning
to leave New York as soon as he finished law school. He said he
would like kids but that he certainly wouldn't have them for at
least a decade—by which point, childbearing would be biologically
challenging for me. And yet . . . I developed big fantasies, while
he developed great impatience to *get it on.* And then we did. And
he called things off a week later. I suppose I shouldn't have been
shocked, but I was devastated.

I felt completely out of control. Much as I wanted to reel myself
in, I couldn't. Instead, I thought about him nonstop for months. I was
leveled. We had so much in common, and such a connection—didn't
we? Why hadn't he thrown caution to the wind for me?

Around that time, I happened to reread *The Aeneid*—which finally
put me on the road to recovery from the lawyer-in-training.

Before I explain why, allow me to take a moment here to say that
I was not reading epic poetry because I'm a pretentious jackass. The
truth is, I respond to books the same way I respond to men: If I'm
not hooked straight away, there's little chance I'll give things a sec-
ond shot. (Not that this strategy hasn't worked against me, I'm sure,
when it comes to both men and books—a topic I discuss in the *Sense
and Sensibility* chapter.) Ancient though *The Aeneid* may be, it turns me
on. The Robert Fitzgerald translation is breathtaking. There's one
stunning extended metaphor after the other, a number of touching

moments, and plenty of great action scenes—not usually my thing but so well depicted by Virgil that it's hard not to dig them. (All the same, I admit that having a handle on the plot makes it much easier to follow. So before you begin reading it, consulting a brief summary might be helpful; they're pretty easy to find online.)

The tragic lovers in the book are mighty Aeneas, a Trojan warrior, and Queen Dido. A few years before they meet, Aeneas and some of his fellow Trojans manage to survive one of the most famous sieges ever, the Trojan Horse massacre. (Beware of Greeks bearing gifts, as the saying goes—especially ones in equine shapes.) Though they fight bravely, Aeneas and co. are forced to flee. He leads his displaced cronies as they sail the high seas; their goal is to reach modern-day Italy; Aeneas has been informed by his goddess mother, Venus, that he's supposed to found Rome there. But the adventurers have a tough time getting where they want to go, because Venus's rival, the goddess Juno, does everything within her power to make life rough for Aeneas. In fact, she'd prevent him from establishing the city if she could, except that the boss of all the gods, Jupiter, won't allow her to go *that* far. So instead she does whatever she can to slow Aeneas down. And at one point, she pulls some strings so that the god of the winds, Aeolus, blows Aeneas and company into a huge storm that washes them up on the shores of Carthage—Dido's turf.

Dido, not your average queen, is an entrepreneurial head of state—the type who might be on the cover of *Fortune* magazine were she alive today. She'd been married to a rich dude who was the love of her life—but her greedy and nefarious brother murdered her man in the hopes of getting his money. Shrewd Dido managed to grab the fortune first and to abscond with it to North Africa, where she set up Carthage. When the Trojans get to town, Dido's loyal subjects, the Carthaginians, like eager worker bees, are erecting new buildings and a fancy temple, putting up gateways, and laying down cobblestone streets. The Trojans' reputation precedes them: Dido has heard about

how courageously they battled the Greeks. So she welcomes them, inviting them to stay in her city for as long as they'd like, saying:

> . . . My life
> Was one of hardship and forced wandering
> Like your own, till in this land at length
> Fortune would have me rest. Through pain I've learned
> To comfort suffering men.

At a big banquet she throws in Aeneas's honor, he captivates everyone with his account of the Trojan War. Dido is understandably charmed by the man; he's a looker with a powerful war-built body, a heavenly glow about him, and charisma to spare. But she wonders if it's proper for her to have the hots for him; shouldn't she put aside her amorous desires and spend the rest of her life being loyal to the memory of her dead husband? When she asks her sister, Anna, for her take on the matter, Anna is basically like, "Dido, would you give me a break? You're too young for that!" Dido responds by saying, more or less, "Yeah, Anna, I guess you're right."

Even if Anna hadn't given her the thumbs-up, any further resistance on Dido's part would've been futile. See, Amor, god of love (who also goes by his Latin name, Cupid), has already injected Dido with his terrible poison; there's nothing she can do to escape her feelings for Aeneas. (And even now—in the year 2012, when we know there's no baby deity in a diaper with a bow and arrow puncturing us with his love potion—sudden infatuations can feel so sudden and powerful that it's easy to see that the ancients thought a meddling god brought them on.)

Love really does a number on Dido; she is so bowled over that she has sex with Aeneas after knowing him a mere two days (by my count). Afterward they live openly as lovers. Dido thinks they're married in all but the legal sense—and assumes Aeneas is on the same

page. But Aeneas hasn't taken any vows. Nor, for that matter, have the two of them discussed the question of exclusivity.

Because they aren't doing anything to hide their affair—on the contrary, they're practically posing for the paparazzi—word gets around that Dido has a new man. (Virgil's description of how rumor travels is unforgettable. In his words, it's like a grotesque multiheaded beast with "as many tongues and buzzing mouths as eyes" who careens throughout the land.) Eventually, even Jupiter hears about what's going on, and he's kind of pissed that Aeneas is dillydallying; that man has Rome to found! So the big kahuna sends his assistant, Mercury, down to Carthage to have a word with the Trojan.

Aeneas gets the point that he needs to be on his way, and fast. But because he actually *does* care for Dido and is nervous about how much he's going to upset her, he decides the best way to handle the whole thing is . . . to just slink away without telling her. (Oh, Aeneas, you might be a brave warrior but, like so many men, you're a big chicken when it comes to matters of the heart.) Unfortunately for him, Dido is not used to such dishonorable treatment, and when she hears that the Trojan ships are being rigged to sail, she furiously confronts Aeneas. "Can our love not hold you?" she demands. "Because of you, I lost my integrity and my good name!"

She goes on to say that if she'd at least gotten pregnant, that might've softened the blow of his departure a little. (Um, what?) At least then, she explains, she'd have something to remember him by. (Getting knocked up by an erotic marauder is the last thing *I*'d want—but to each her own, I guess. Queens can probably afford a nanny or two.) Instead she feels "utterly defeated, utterly bereft."

Her agonized speech moves Aeneas, though he does his best to hide how deeply he feels for her. Worried that letting himself get carried away won't make his departure easier for either one of them, he tells Dido that she truly means a lot to him, and that as long as he is alive, his memory of her will never pale—but that he has an empire

to found, like it or not. As he puts it: "I sail for Italy not of my own free will."

If you want to know how Dido handles it after he sails away, prepare yourself for a SPOILER ALERT! Right now! Because she commits hara-kiri. Yep—kills herself. I wish I'd been around back then to say to her, "Hey, Dido! It's not you—it's him!" Instead I'll tell *you*: Please don't take it too personally if a guy with big ideas about his future says he can't be in a relationship with you. Plenty of men feel called to certain paths just as much as Aeneas felt called by Jupiter—and as they march toward Rome, they often mistreat queenly ladies, leaving broken hearts in their paths. So just like Dido shouldn't have—and I shouldn't have—don't take it personally if a demigod dumps you. He sails not of his own free will.

Jack says:

Maura, yeah, poor Dido; as lame excuses for dumping someone go, I need to sail off and found Italy really is among the worst. I do love how she tells him off, though, after she catches him trying to sneak out without saying good-bye:

> *I do not*
> *refute your words. I do not keep you back.*
> *Go then, before the winds, to Italy.*
> *Seek out your kingdom overseas; indeed,*
> *if there be pious powers still, I hope*
> *that you will drink your torments to the lees*
> *among sea rocks and, drowning, often cry*
> *the name of Dido.*

This is one of my favorite disses in the whole *Norton Anthology*. Go, girl! You tell him!

THE TAMING
OF THE . . .
WHO?

The Seduction Process

SCORIN' PIECE

Tolstoy's Surefire Way to Be Wanted by Everyone

ACCORDING TO JACK

I have to say, at first glance, the title of this chapter strikes even me as unlikely. Who would think that *War and Peace*, one of the longest novels ever written and generally thought of as one of the most boring (though it's far, far from), would be a veritable tutorial in man-landing and how to be luscious?

But shelve your doubts with your wedge espadrilles, because as it turns out, Tolstoy himself was quite the womanizer. He knew a LOT about what is appealing in the fairer sex, and true enough—turn the pages of his great novel (*Anna Karenina*, I hate to break it to you, isn't his masterpiece) and you'll get a surefire program in the A-#1 secret to how to be alluring. And trust me; it works.

There are three principal characters in *War and Peace*: Pierre, Andrei, and Natasha, and both the first two utterly fall for the third. The beguiling Natasha is based on the younger sister of the woman Tolstoy himself wed, because when he was in his thirties, he spent a lot of time at the household of the Behrs family, flirting with and enjoying the admiration of the three sisters. Everyone thought he would propose to the oldest, Liza, but out of the blue he proposed to the middle one, Sophia—pretty sneaky, sis! (Tolstoy's biographer

speculates that Sophia, despite not being the most attractive or out-going of the three, had some sort of beguiling sexual energy that Tolstoy could not resist.) The proposal came as a thunderbolt, and Tolstoy insisted that they marry two weeks later. But his fascination with the youngest Behrs daughter, Tatyana, lasted his lifetime. My armchair diagnosis is that Tolstoy, like many writers (ahem), was not the most secure of all individuals, and while he was utterly captivated by Tatyana, he was a little afraid of her as well. Not having the co-jones to propose to her himself, instead he created a female character out of her and had his two major protagonists do so.

So, what was Natasha's secret? Let's examine the evidence. When we first meet her, she's a girl of twelve described as "a little bit of quicksilver"—hinting at her sparkle and unwillingness to be con-tained. Soon enough, though, she becomes the belle of the Moscow balls, a creature made to dance and laugh and flirt. She is both enrap-turing and enraptured, "not enamored of anyone in particular, but of everyone. She was in love with everyone on whom her eyes happened to fall for that moment. 'Oh how lovely it is!' she kept saying."

And though the first part of the quote might suggest flightiness—the young Natasha *is* a little on the inconstant side—Tolstoy paints the latter part of her character with a finer brush, the side of her that brings inordinate appreciation and enthusiasm to life. A hundred pages later, Natasha will repeat her phrase "Oh how lovely it is"—this time in reference to the moonlight-basked panorama outside her bedroom window. "Sonya, Sonya," she calls to her sister, thrusting her head out the window. "Look what a moon! Oh, how lovely! . . . I feel like squatting down on my heels, putting my arms round my knees like this, tight—as tight as can be—and flying away!"

Prince Andrei, a serious man who thought he had given up on the pleasures of life, hears her from below, and "all at once such an unexpected turmoil of youthful thoughts and hopes, contrary to the whole tenor of his life, surged up in his heart."

This is the effect joie de vivre has on the people around you: They share in it, feeling more engaged, more alive and vital, like crocuses rising up to see the sun. When you are joyful, when you say yes to life and have fun and project positivity all around you, you become a sun in the center of every constellation, and people want to be near you.

Natasha is just such a life force, as we see in the vital scene a few hundred pages later, when, despite being a woman, she participates in a wild chase on horseback through the woods and countryside in pursuit of a fleeing she-wolf. The hunt is led by a woodsman they call Uncle, and when it is over, they retire to Uncle's cabin, where Natasha has amazed all the men by having participated, sitting sidesaddle on her horse and neither falling nor being scared.

It is at Uncle's cabin that Natasha shows her truest colors, her remarkable gift for sucking the marrow out of life. A diverse hunter's meal is served and she eats everything, thinking that all the food "seemed to her the best in the world." (And can I say in passing that when a woman has no dietary restrictions, that's *fantastic*. It pretty much signals to me that she is game for things in general, whereas the more things a woman won't eat, the more I sense she's going to restrict herself in other domains as well—no fun!) Then the music starts, a peasant-y rustic kind of tune, and Natasha rises to dance, even though none of the nobles present think she'll know how. But she dances, and "the spirit and the movements were the very ones— inimitable, unteachable, Russian . . . The slender, graceful countess, reared in silks and velvets, in another world than hers . . . was yet able to understand all that was in Anisya [Uncle's servant] and in Anisya's father and mother and aunt, and in every Russian man and woman."

I hope you can hear the pride Tolstoy puts in these lines, pride both in his country and its spirit, and how that spirit manifested itself in this character and the young woman she was based on. He loved Russia because it was a vital nation, full of verve and juice, and he loved Tatyana/Natasha for the same reasons. So when he has her

dance the dance of the people, he's trying to tell us that her joy and approach to life transcends the situation and transforms every situation. She makes it hers by sharing it with all of us.

I, too, fell quickly under Natasha's spell, despite having spent much of my life being Natasha's opposite: saying no, being risk-averse, denying myself pleasure, watching from the side instead of participating, thinking that all that stuff—whatever it was, ice-skating or drinking or dating—was for others, not for me. It took until my twenties for me to realize what a horrible way to live that was, and it's taken me all the time since to try to undo my long-established habits. Now I think I've learned from my mistakes, and it will be my life goal to get my children to dance and sing and embrace life.

And now that I'm older, I've also figured out the kind of woman I like best: It's obviously women like Natasha, the kind Tolstoy liked, the kind who help us connect to the joy and vitality in things. Women like this, women who are really alive, are the most captivating of all; they are making the most out of living, and they help you do it, too.

Chapter 15

SEX AND SENSIBILITY

Are Relationships That Start with Wild Passion Doomed?

ACCORDING TO MAURA

Before starting to work on this book, I'm fairly certain I'd never read a Jane Austen novel all the way through. Sure, just about everyone I know, male and female alike, raves about her (with the very notable exception of Jack). And clearly, Lady Jane has a huge following, not only among readers but creative types: *Bridget Jones's Diary* was Helen Fielding's wildly successful and very funny re-creation of *Pride and Prejudice*; Amy Heckerling's witty movie *Clueless* was inspired by *Emma*; and Quirk Books is laughing all the way to the bank with its Austen parody series, comprised of titles like *Pride & Prejudice & Zombies*.

Nonetheless—maybe it's a contrarian streak I have, but—the brief forays I'd made into Austen-land left me wondering why people were so into her. She has a decent sense of humor; I'll give you that. She has some strong-willed heroines. And Austen sure knows her way around a plot, too. But her characters never seemed that complex or interesting to me—so many society girls, so obsessed with marriage! Her stories are heavy on machinations, fairly light on psychological insights and vivid descriptions; as such, I didn't feel like I was going

to learn anything very meaningful about life or humanity by reading Jane Austen.

But knowing that many of you probably love her—as plenty of my friends do—I felt like I needed to give the old girl one more shot. I decided to go with *Sense and Sensibility* mainly because I'd never so much as peeked at it, whereas I *had* attempted *Pride and Prejudice, Emma,* and *Mansfield Park.* Plus, since it was Austen's first published novel, it seemed as good a place to begin (again) as any.

No more than a few pages in, I remembered all the things I disliked about her—the haughty voice; the dissatisfying third-person narrator; the young female characters whose biggest problems in life, it seemed, were not being able to afford as many maids as they would like, and trying to decide who the hell they should marry. Nonetheless, because I felt I owed her more than a fair shot, I pushed through . . . and after a few chapters, I found the book hard to put down. I was sucked in! I didn't want to sleep at night, for the reading!

The story revolves around two sisters, the Dashwoods: Elinor, the older, more sensible one, and Marianne, younger and far more impetuous. Marianne, something of a drama queen, wears her heart on her sleeve and spends much of the novel determined to give free reign to her emotions at all times, no matter how uncomfortable her histrionics make other people. Elinor, on the other hand, is always eager to conform to societal norms, even if doing so means squelching her true feelings, a bit like Jane Eyre might have. Austen clearly prefers the Elinor types to the Mariannes. As she writes: "Elinor . . . possessed a strength of understanding, and coolness of judgment, which qualified her . . . to be the counselor of her mother . . . her feelings were strong but she knew how to govern them . . . [Marianne] was sensible and clever; but eager in everything; her sorrows, her joys, could have no moderation. She was generous, amiable, interesting: she was everything but prudent."

(Frankly, though I see the benefit of being an Elinor, I'm probably

more of a Marianne. Though I'd never cry in public or abruptly depart a dinner party if one of the guests said something upsetting, the way Marianne would, I also wouldn't go out of my way to flatter or please people I didn't respect just because they happen to be in my wider social circle, the way Elinor does. I quite *like* Elinor—she's the kind of rational, reasonable, responsible person who would make for a good friend—and it would probably benefit me if I *could* be like her; I'm just not sure that will ever be possible.)

Elinor is in love with Edward Ferrars, a guy who is "not handsome," and has "manners [that] required intimacy to make them pleasing." Not exactly the kind of description that would jump out at you while perusing the Craigslist personal ads, is it? Add lack of ambition (which is almost as bad as an excess of it) to his list of less-than-attractive qualities, and Edward doesn't exactly sound like a catch—though he *is* respectable in the sense that he has a system of personal values to which he diligently adheres. Still, he comes off like such a stick-in-the-mud that I had trouble caring too much about the fate of his entanglement with Elinor—which his meddling family is determined to put an end to because they think she isn't wealthy enough for him.

Marianne falls for a much more charismatic, emotive, flirtatious type—a good-looking young man named Willoughby who easily charms just about everyone he meets, herself included. Though he gives Marianne every reason to believe she has a special place in his heart, he begins to behave in a way that's so unpredictable and disappointing that it's hard for Elinor—and the reader—not to suspect he's a player. But Marianne has eyes only for him, despite the fact that a more eligible and respectable (not to mention wealthy) man named Colonel Brandon has a huge crush on her. Though Brandon isn't bad looking, at thirty-six he's roughly twice as old as she is, and she doesn't feel physically attracted to him. Moreover, she doesn't have the same kind of bubbly conversations with the good colonel that she

does with Willoughby; the older man is much more reserved and serious than the younger.

But *Elinor* isn't bothered by Brandon's relative taciturnity, and she's impressed by how responsible he is to those he loves. In fact, the two of *them* slowly but steadily become the best of friends and have the most emotionally serious exchanges of all the male-female duos in the book. They get along *so* well that I quickly found myself rooting for them to end up together—especially after we learn that Edward is already engaged to another chick! (At the same time, I had to wonder if Brandon and Elinor had anything other than platonic feelings for each other; there didn't seem to be much chemistry between them.)

Since I don't want to reveal too much more about what happens, I won't tell you what transpires between Elinor and Edward, or whether Willoughby turns out to be a scoundrel or a sweetheart. However, I think it's necessary to reveal that, much to my amazement and disappointment, Marianne ends up with Colonel Brandon. Wrong sister, if you ask me. Perhaps even more unforgivably, their union is announced way too suddenly, without a proper buildup of how Marianne's feelings might have been transformed from platonic to erotic, from relatively indifferent to interested. Austen plops it on us without much more advance warning than the following hasty paragraphs:

> [W]ith a knowledge so intimate of his goodness—with a conviction of his fond attachment to herself, which at last, though long after it was observable to everybody else—burst on her—what could she do?

> [She] was born to an extraordinary fate . . . with no sentiment superior to strong esteem and lively friendship, [she had decided] voluntarily to give her hand to [Brandon].

"An extraordinary fate"? Uh, wouldn't it have been more accurate to say: "She settled for a nice guy—and they probably had pretty bland sex"?

Maybe that's a little harsh, but I used to think a strong initial physical attraction was necessary for any couple who wants to make it through the long haul. Didn't an early sense of awe about each other change the brain circuitry in some crucial way that helped spouses continue to find each other stimulating, even after they'd known each other for years? And give them the extra push they needed to get through hard times?

A study described in the 2010 book *Click: The Magic of Instant Connections* indicates that there might be something to my theory—but that Austen might have a point as well. One thousand couples—who'd been married, on average, twenty-five years—were asked to fill out questionnaires full of probing questions about their marriages. (Husbands and wives responded separately, after being assured by the psychologists in charge that their spouses wouldn't see their answers.) The researchers wanted to examine the impact that "clicking"—or feeling an almost immediate sense of passion and intimacy—had on long-term relationships. They wondered: Had couples who'd felt an instantaneous spark fared best? Were they happier and healthier than the married people who'd been longtime friends before they'd started dating? What about those, in a third category, who weren't friends first and hadn't felt an immediate connection either, but developed serious feelings for each other during a traditional courtship (the kind that involved going on numerous dates and only gradually becoming more serious)?

Contrary to my expectations, the psychologists who'd designed the experiment hypothesized that the people in the last two groups—the ones whose sense of romantic attachment developed slowly—would have stronger, healthier relationships after twenty-five years than those who'd begun their relationships with a feeling of giddy

mutual infatuation. (Jane Austen might have surmised the same.) What the researchers found, however, surprised them: There was virtually no difference in terms of commitment and closeness among the three groups. What's more, though the spouses whose love needed time to grow ended up with more common interests, those who felt enamored right away were more likely to say they felt their relationships were still "magical"; they also reported thinking about their spouses frequently during the day. In other words, the people in the first group—the clickers!—remained more hot for their spouses, all those years later, than those in the other groups.

The findings also surprised *me*. I'd assumed that anyone who "settled," as Marianne did, would end up with a marriage that wasn't very happy or satisfying in the long run. As it happens, though, people who didn't start with serious crushes were able to turn feelings of mutual respect and admiration into long-lasting, meaningful romantic relationships—and, after twenty-five years, they didn't seem to resent each other.

So what does this mean? That *Sense and Sensibility* contains a good lesson: An interdependency built slowly with a person who cares deeply for you and wants to make things work can turn out very nicely indeed. And while flame-throwing erotic attachments have the none-too-shabby advantage of being more likely to remain mind-blowing for the long haul, I wonder how many of them actually *make* it to the twenty-five-year mark; I wouldn't be surprised if plenty go kaput within a year or two. It's certainly interesting to note that Ted Huston, a psychology professor at the University of Texas at Austin, announced in a 2009 report that the two kinds of couples most likely to divorce are those who have had very rocky courtships *and* those who have had extremely passionate, fabulous ones. In other words, a relationship that takes some time to get rolling is less of a gamble, more of a sure thing; less exciting but more sage.

Of course, being reasonable doesn't appeal much to the Marianne

in me; I still find it difficult to so much as go on a second date with a guy if I'm not strongly attracted to him. But the older I get, the more I see the appeal of the world's Colonel Brandons—and I urge all of you other Mariannes to give them a shot. Taking it slow and steady with a levelheaded man can be a storybook romance in its own right.

Jack says:

Maura, well, this one strikes a little close to the bone. Two of my three longest and most loving relationships were virtual live-together affairs after the first date (in one of them, she actually moved in the next day), and the third one began with the kind of fireworks I barely knew existed—but your prediction was mostly true; even though two of them passed the two-year mark, all three did eventually come to an end.

I would still like to think that early pyrotechnics aren't necessarily a bad sign, that people who really dig each other from the get-go can then try to work out the stuff that makes not just good chemistry but a good relationship happen (i.e., figuring out how to deal with conflict, difficulty, etc. Good sex can give you a lot of motivation to figure those things out, but it certainly doesn't guarantee you'll be able to).

So, yes, I don't think you should have to hold back at the beginning of a relationship, but I do think you should realize that all that fun and good feeling isn't going to be enough. You still have to do the work; sadly, there's no way around that. But when it's the right person at the right time, the work will feel very worthwhile.

Chapter 16

REMEMBRANCE OF
THINGS PASSED ON

Don't Try to Get Back Together!

ACCORDING TO JACK

We've all been there: drunkenly dialing up an ex boyfriend or girlfriend—or texting, emailing, even ringing his or her doorbell, God forbid—hoping to get back together, forgetting all the bad stuff and just wanting more of the good.

But plaintively pleading with your former lover to start things up again is almost never a good idea. Not only do you give him grounds to mock you for breaking up in the first place (if you were the one who did so) of the "See, I knew you'd come crawling back!" variety. But, as anyone who's actually ever gotten back together with an ex can tell you, you *do* still have problems, usually exactly the same ones as before, and the things that made you break up the first time have a strong chance of making you break up again. I've tried a number of times to sew back together sundered threads, but there should be a saying along the lines of "once broken up, forever broken." Them's just the facts, Jack, and even an enormous amount of love, hope, and effort aren't necessarily enough to re-glue the vase and get the thing to actually hold water again.

But, really, what's a more human thing to do than want to try again? Hope springs eternal, right? And in our weaker—or, as I

mentioned above, more sauced—moments, we are all subject to deep, intense longings that dupe both memory and logic and lead us to consider renewing things with an old lover. I remember back in college being at a party and tipsily going up to a former girlfriend saying, "Can't we just pretend that we don't have any problems?" (Maybe not the worst strategy; I've seen marriages that operate that way . . .). Her response was to laugh me away and, in truth, that was exactly what I needed; the thought *was* pretty laughable, if well-intentioned. I simply needed to sleep it off and go back to my right mind.

Literature also abounds with characters whose longings get the best of them, but when it comes to getting back together with exes, Marcel Proust provides more case-study evidence than perhaps any other classic writer. The plot of his 3,300-page *Remembrance of Things Past* circles back on itself time and again, and many of the relationships also circle back as well, showing in detail the trials and tribulations of attempting to regain lost love.

Remembrance of Things Past is a conjoined series of autobiographical novels, and its protagonist—also named Marcel—has relations with a number of the women (though they were men in reality) that fail to work out over the course of the seven volumes. Marcel is one of literature's great spoiled brats, and when things go south, he is typically derisive and dismissive of all his former lovers. He cautions himself (and us) against trying to mend things—but then he does so anyway! In fact, the young and randy Marcel gets back together (or tries to) with Gilberte, Andrée, and, most important, Albertine, and it is this last that concerns us the most.

Albertine is *Remembrance of Things Past*'s femme fatale (the novel's sixth volume, *Albertine disparue*, is named after her, and in a novel *so* self-involved as this one, anyone—and of course she's the only one—to get a volume named after her clearly left a mark). She is introduced in the second volume, *A l'ombre de jeunes filles en fleurs* (in the shadow of young girls a-blossom), as one of a pack of insouciant

female bicyclers at the beachside resort town where Marcel, due to various physical ailments, is taking a doctor-recommended therapeutic visit—with his mother, of course. *Quite* the mama's boy, our Marcel!

After many fits and starts, Marcel and Albertine eventually become an item, but they couldn't be much more volatile, breaking up and starting over repeatedly, leading up to the scene I'd like to analyze below (which, for those of you scoring at home, happens to be the earliest high-literature example of a booty call).

At this still-middle point of the story, Marcel and Albertine are in one of their many ambiguous phases. But Marcel's horniness gets the best of him, so he buys her tickets to the opera and tells her to call him after and come over (at the end of the nineteenth century, the telephone was quite a new invention, though Marcel had put one in his bedroom for just such purposes, naughty little man).

Marcel's reasons for wanting Albertine to come over are pretty much what most of us feel when we try to hook back up with exes— if we were honest with ourselves. He readily admits (to the reader, though not to Albertine) that he "was not the least in love with her, in asking her to come this evening." Instead he was merely "yielding to a purely sensual desire." Later, having waited impatiently for hours (drinking all the while), he gushes, "I was tortured by the incessant recurrence of my longing, ever more anxious and never gratified, for the sound of a call, having arrived at the culminating point of a tortuous ascent through the coils of my lonely anguish." Sound a little drunk and sappy to you, too? Maybe even a little familiar? (Sure does to me!)

But then Albertine *does* call: "I'm not disturbing you, ringing you up at this hour?" she says coquettishly. He retorts with the obligatory "No, not at all" and then asks with feigned indifference, "Are you coming round?"

They do the standard game players' little back-and-forth power

play, but at the point when he thinks she really won't come, he begins to feel emotions it's easy to fall prey to, those which lead us to make decisions we will regret later. Proust calls it "the longing to see again the velvet-soft face," but even at this point he recognizes the shallowness of his desire, acknowledging that "this terrible need of a person . . . to combine and form a single element with the other . . . had for its voluptuous object only the colored surface, the flesh-pink bloom of a flower on the sea shore, was one that often results simply in creating (in the chemical sense) a new body, which may last only a few moments."

Sadly, in many get-back-togethers, Proust's description is pretty much on the mark; there *are* weak moments when we can't help but covet a shared body, that sense of closeness and comfort, the freedom from problems and reality—even if the object is completely inappropriate. What we forget, of course, is that reality will always win out, and the pleasure might "last only a few moments." How many people have awakened in the arms of the ex they drunk-dialed and thought, *God, what have I done? Don't tell me I'm back in this again? How will I escape?*

The key of course is to remember how fickle memory is and how much it can dance to the tune the heart sets it. Here more than ever Proust is our mentor (he is literature's all-time authority on memory), reminding us that "the images selected by memory are as arbitrary, as narrow, as elusive as those which the imagination had formed and reality had destroyed." In other words, we recall what serves to promote whatever partial truths our daydreams (or alcohol-induced thoughts) are trying to sell us.

But life tends to destroy these daydreams, and it normally doesn't take much time. Proust knows it, too, saying that "a fresh reality" (by which he means whatever you end up with when you get back together) "will perhaps make us forget, detest even, the desires on account of which we set out on our journey." I.e., not only does it normally not work out, you can even end up getting furious at the

heartfelt or merely physical promptings that led you back there in the first place.

For Marcel and Albertine, this reunion and various others after are no more successful. They continue to find themselves in a vicious spiral of nostalgia, return, and renewed disaster. Proust sums it up in a wonderful phrase, saying that "with the perturbations of memory are linked the intermittencies of the heart." And, yes, memory *can* be fickle, and the heart *can* be intermittent—it's painful to acknowledge, but we do well to remain aware that while old embers of love might spark anew, so, too, will come the cold rains that doused them in the first place.

So no matter how much you long for your former flame, take out a piece of paper and write down all the reasons it didn't work out the first time. Be as thorough as you can. How many of those have changed? How many are likely to change?

We might want to think that the second time around is going to be better, but the sad truth is that people don't change that much, and the renewed attempt is likely to be just another turn of the same old wheel.

THE BLABBERS KARAMAZOV

The Dangers of Revealing Too Much Too Soon

ACCORDING TO MAURA

If you've made it this far into our book, you've probably started to notice that I don't keep too many secrets about my personal life. And while I think that's a fine thing—kinda necessary, really—for a modern-day essay writer, it sure has hurt my dating life. Probably *a lot. . . .*

But before I talk any more about TMI, permit me to tell you about a novel that I love dearly: Fyodor Dostoevksy's tour de force *The Brothers Karamazov*. Recently, when I lugged it with me to the gym so I could reread it on the StairMaster, one of my fellow exercisers jokingly asked if he could borrow the book to do his arm curls. Hardy har har. It's true that the novel is so heavy with sentences that it could be used to anchor a small ship. But it doesn't just sit there like a deadweight. It *moves*—drawing you in with some of the most vivid, nutty, manic characters in the history of literature, keeping you on the edge of your couch after a murder occurs and the motivations of all the possible suspects are slowly revealed. Admittedly, it's not till the second half that things really go *full-steam ahead*. But throughout, the novel keeps you onboard with all its twisting and turning and delightful explorations into the complicated ways in which love and

hate, hope and despair, self-destructiveness and the perpetuation of identity can coexist. Sure, it's about twice as long as Dostoevsky's next most-celebrated book, *Crime and Punishment*, but it's also about ten times as good—with more humor, more action, more emotion, more transformation, more redemption.

Given the title, you won't be surprised to hear that the book centers around three brothers—and if you're like me, it'll be hard for you to decide which one you have the biggest crush on. Is it fresh-faced Alexei, the youngest and most innocent? He's a monk in training who experiences a crisis of faith when his religious mentor dies; he begins to think he should marry a crippled girl, partly because he's very fond of her, but mainly because it seems like the right thing to do. Or would you prefer the brilliant intellectual Ivan? The most practical and rational of the three, he's making a name for himself in the writing world; at times, he comes off as cold and calculating, but he can also be a man of powerful emotions—evidenced by the deep love he feels for a forsaken woman. Or what about their wildly passionate and rather manic half brother, Dmitri? A former soldier given to profligate displays of affection, he's always wearing his heart on his sleeve—particularly after he falls for a certain young lady with such ferocious abandon that he seems willing to ruin his life for her. Knowing that all three of the boys lost their mothers when they were quite young *and* that their father is an unparalleled asshole (though he's also a hilarious and unforgettable creation) will make you feel even more affection for them.

Believe it or not, however, it's the asshole himself, Papa Fyodor Karamazov—a miserly, lecherous, unprincipled landowner—whom I want to focus on here. About the best you can say for him is that he doesn't physically abuse his family . . . although he does pretty much everything else. He steals money from his first wife, for example, and when she runs off, exasperated with his greed, only to die in ruin, he abandons their son (Dmitri). In short order, he

remarries a sixteen-year-old orphan girl with suicidal tendencies and proceeds to have orgies with other women in front of her. She begins experiencing terrible fits of hysteria that eventually kill her, at which point Papa K. promptly starts ignoring the two sons that *she* bore him—i.e., Ivan and Alexei. (All three boys end up being raised by a hodgepodge of kind servants, relatives, and do-gooders.) But Papa K. isn't finished yet: Next he impregnates a mentally disabled young woman. (Or, at least everyone's pretty sure he did it, though he won't admit to it.) The helpless girl dies during childbirth. Papa K. never acknowledges that the child who survives is his, but he does allow the same servants who raised his other sons to take the fourth boy in. Once that bastard, Smerdyakov—an epileptic with an evil side—comes of age, Papa K. indentures him as his personal chef and lackey. If all that weren't bad enough, when Dmitri reaches adulthood, he falls for that woman I mentioned earlier—a mischievous, manipulative siren named Grushenka—only to find his weasel of a father viciously competing with him for her affections. The two clash so violently over Grushenka that homicidal emotions arise, leading to devastating results for both of them: Papa K. is murdered, and most fingers point at Dmitri, who has raved many times about killing the jerk.

Surprisingly, however, thanks to Dostoevsky's power as a writer, it's possible at moments to feel some degree of understanding (if not quite sympathy) for Papa K. Certainly, I understood where he was coming from during one of his most appalling public performances, in a scene involving him and his three legitimate sons. Alexei, concerned about the growing tension between his father and older brother, asks the renowned holy man Father Zossima to preside over a family counseling session; he requests that Ivan attend. The wanna-be monk is somewhat optimistic that Zossima will forge a reconciliation between Papa and Dmitri. Yet he also fears his father will screw everything up and embarrass them, the way he has so many times before.

Ivan—who despises his father about as much as Dmitri does, though he conceals his antipathy better—is worried, too.

The appointed hour arrives, and Alexei, Ivan, Papa, and Zossima wait in the priest's chambers for tardy Dmitri. As they pass the time, wondering when he will arrive, Papa K. assumes center stage—and his kids' worst anxieties are realized. He recounts ribald stories, remarks zanily to the dignified Zossima that there might be "an unclean spirit" inside of him, rambles maniacally, and generally makes a great performance out of what Zossima calls his " 'verbal incontinence.' " As his sons hang their heads, humiliated by the sociopathically disrespectful way he carries on, Papa K. devilishly asks Zossima if he, too, is offended—mainly because he's trying to stir up more trouble. Rather than take the bait, Zossima tells Papa to do his best to relax and feel comfortable. "Above all," Zossima instructs him, "do not be ashamed of yourself, for that is the cause of everything."

It sure is!

Zossima's perspicacity impresses Papa K. "That remark you just made . . . it's as if you pierced me right through and read inside me," the old man tells the priest. "That is exactly how it all seems to me, when I walk into a room, that I'm lower than anyone else, and that everyone takes me for a buffoon, so [I think] 'Why not, indeed, play the buffoon . . . !' That's why I'm a buffoon, I'm a buffoon out of shame, great elder, out of shame. I act up just because I'm insecure. If only I were sure, when I came in [to the room], that everyone would take me at once for the most pleasant and intelligent of men—oh, Lord! what a good man I'd be!"

Strange though this may sound, I spent most of my twenties acting somewhat like Papa Karamazov just about every time I went on a date. Expecting that I'd never be able to sufficiently impress whatever guy I was about to meet up with, I'd often feel the need to calm my nerves beforehand with a shot or two; sometimes I'd even sneak into the bathroom of the coffee shop or bar where we were

having our rendezvous so I could slurp straight from the fifth of whiskey that I was carrying in my purse. (My reasoning: Only an alcoholic would order a shooter immediately upon arriving, right?) In retrospect, I'm not sure how much that *helped*, but it certainly loosened me up. I'd return to my seat and launch almost immediately into a prattling session. I'd tell one crazy story after the other—like the one about that New Year's Eve when I kissed a cabbie, or the one about the young drug dealer I met at a bar in Berlin, or the one about that night when a limo driver picked me up near Lincoln Center and offered me some cocaine off the clipboard he was snorting from. . . .

Talking that way, as perhaps I don't need to tell you, doesn't exactly put you on the fast track for getting a boyfriend. And yet I wish someone *had* told *me!* Instead, I carried on like a Karamazovian buffoon for years and years before I began to slowly change myself.

Why did I talk so much? Part of it was that I thought such escapades made me sound glamorous, wild, and daring—like a person living an interesting, edgy, New York City life! Full of adventure and unusual experiences! And yet that's not the whole story. The literary critic James Wood, in his essay on Dostoevsky from his collection *The Irresponsible Self*, gets a bit closer to explaining it. Many of Dostoevsky's characters, Wood writes, "even the very godless ones like Fyodor Karamazov, live under the mottled shadow of [religion] . . . Above all, their actions are comprehensible only and finally as efforts to confess, to reveal themselves, to be known." In other words, you might say, both Papa K. and I had guilty consciences; he, a character created by a very religious writer who was preoccupied with the ideals of the Eastern Orthodox Church, and I, a character created by two very religious parents who were preoccupied with Catholicism. We told the truth about what we did in part because we hoped we'd be forgiven.

Or, at least, *I* sure did. In my early years, I really wanted to be a good girl, but the strictures of the Catholic Church are so severe that

even when I didn't mean to, I was sinning all the time. *Thoughts*, for a Catholic, can be sinful; we're prohibited not just from stealing and cheating but from *coveting*, for crying out loud. I did fairly well when it came to controlling my actions, but preventing myself from having verboten cogitations was another matter. Of course, at a certain point in my youth, I started to think Catholicism was nonsense. And yet—to paraphrase a popular line from *The Usual Suspects*—though I no longer believed in God, I still *feared* him. Put another way, it was easy to remove the God algorithm from the software in my brain, much harder to eliminate a subtler bug: the idea that because I had "bad" thoughts, I was a bad, bad girl. When your mind works that way, it encourages you to do some bad things; on some level, you start to feel it's not worth even *trying* to be good, when no matter what, you'll always be bad.

So I had one naughty adventure after another. And I confessed them to my dates in great detail because I wanted to be forgiven—or even better, to be accepted. Not for who I *wasn't*, but for who I was, warts and all. (Luckily no genital ones.) Nonetheless—after many years of wincing introspection—I began to realize how uncomfortable my drunken tell-alls were making *me*. And while my party-girl escapades might have been *one* of the things that made me the person I was, plenty of other qualities—like my love for literature—came to seem a lot more crucial to my personality. They definitely inspired much better first-date conversations.

Slowly, I started to appreciate that it *wasn't* actually necessary to reveal my most exotic misbehaviors and deepest, darkest secrets to a man *the very first night I met him*—and the more I held back, the more often I found myself being asked on second dates, and third ones, even fourths. I began to understand how much easier it is to accept someone's shortcomings, faults, and the things they struggle with *after* you've begun to like them for their better qualities. "Being yourself" on a first date is important, of course—but that certainly doesn't

mean it's advisable to be your *worst* self straight out of the gate, the way I was for so many years.

Recently, I said almost exactly that to a new friend of mine—a very attractive, startlingly intelligent, hilariously witty woman in her midthirties. We'd been talking about how hard dating can be, and she said something about how she almost *never* got to a third date with any man she was interested in, let alone a second. *Hmm,* I thought; *sounds familiar.* So I pried, and one thing led to another, and eventually she said, "I feel like a guy needs to know immediately that I take antidepressants, because if he can't deal with that, it'll never work out anyway. Why not get it over with quickly?"

For all the reasons I just gave!

As I told her, plenty of people still think that taking psychotropic medication is a sign that someone is off her rocker or will be difficult to deal with (when in fact it's actually a sign that she is taking good care of her health). It's not unusual for people to make snap (if unfair) judgments about the folks who take them. What's more, even a guy who doesn't think being on head meds is such a big deal may find it a bit discomfiting if you blurt out within thirty minutes of meeting him that you are. Your inability to keep from discussing them, more than the fact of the prescription itself, might make you seem a bit unhinged. So let him see how awesome—and stable and sane—you are *before* you inform him that Wellbutrin helps keep you that way.

And if he's cool with that? Then you have my blessing to tell him about that time you kissed the cab driver, too.

ALL'S WELL THAT ENDS WITH AN ORGASM

Ah, Yes, the Sex

TROPIC OF ROMANCER

Henry Miller Knows How to Get It On

ACCORDING TO JACK

I heard a story once, told by a friend who knew the daughter of a famously beautiful, ultrasuccessful female singer (whose heyday was in the '70s) about the man the singer called "the best lay in Hollywood." She then named one of our most famous male actors—shock!—and I found it somehow fascinating to know who took that particular cake (just as I was intrigued later to hear stories of the apparently preposterous size of a certain classic comedian's manhood—and, yes, I'm a guy; I care about these things).

To avoid being sued for all I own (pretty much just moldy books), I won't reveal the name, but even more fascinating than hearing *who* was the top shag in Tinseltown was hearing *why*. The singer said it wasn't technique, size, endurance or any of the things we often think will make a man (or anyone) good in bed; no, it turns out the simple reason was that "you could tell he liked it more. He was just more into it than anyone else." He loved it, and that made you love it. What a trick!

Now, I'm not saying that mere enthusiasm by itself will turn any old Joe into Casanova (or Jill into Cleopatra), because we all know that the selfish, in-their-own-world-and-you-could-be-anyone lover

is one of the world's worst. But, all else being equal, the person who gives off gratitude, whose enjoyment and into-it-ness is really palpable, makes it a lot more fun for the person he or she is with. The difference between having a hellcat or a cold fish as your partner can hardly be overstated.

Now, there's an age-old question of what gives more pleasure: getting what you want or being wanted? We tend to think that the answer depends primarily on the gender of the person answering, with most guys simply wanting to get their desires gratified and many women getting more fulfillment out of being desired. But I think the answers are much more overlayed and mixed than that—for both genders. Obviously more and more women are getting better at knowing consciously what it is they want and then actively going and getting it (whoo hoo!); what's less discussed is how much men like to feel wanted and how much that can improve the sexual experience for them.

I suppose it's not surprising that many women don't realize the degree to which the simple fact of loving sex can make the act great for both parties. So many media messages discourage girls and women from embracing their libidos, as if you should be ashamed of feeling desires and have to keep anyone from ever knowing (it seems like it's even worse in Japan, where manga cartoon after manga cartoon depicts the women apologizing for feeling pleasure but then not being able to keep from showing it physically—a telling dichotomy, if you ask me). Women are told to act hard to get, not to pursue, to keep quiet during sex, not to be "a screamer" or "too loud" (but what's the threat?), and on and on.

The result, of course, is that many women *try* to be repressed, and sex as a whole suffers from it. Guys don't feel as wanted; they don't realize how into it the women actually are or can be, and neither gender is aware how much is being lost in the equation.

That's why we have to read more Henry Miller.

Old Hank, as I've written elsewhere and as anyone who's cracked any of his covers knows, is pretty much all about *un*-repression.

Famous for the raciness of his novels (and the lack of checks he put on his ego as well as his id), Miller has long been thought of as the great literary voice of the uninhibited. *Tropic of Cancer*, his most famous novel, was banned in America for obscenity from its publication in the 1930s until Barney Rosset of Grove Press championed it in the 1950s and won the legal battle to publish it stateside in 1961.

And, yes, *Tropic of Cancer* has graphic descriptions of genitalia and what people do with them, but in some ways that's not the part, I don't think, that pressed the censors' buttons. My guess is that it was more the graphic descriptions of *pleasure*, both for men and for women, that really bugged them. (You've heard the quip about puritanism being the haunting fear that someone somewhere is having more fun? Bingo.)

So while it might have been the anatomical parts that technically got *Cancer* banned, it's the juice that really caused the ruckus—and that juice is exactly why we should read him today. Miller clearly was a man like the famous actor I described above; he was *into* it—and he liked his women to be into it as well.

As such he gives us repeated tutorials in precisely why we *want* to be with physical/libidinal enthusiasts—and therefore why we shouldn't be so critical of potential lovers who have, say, a few extra miles on their tires. There's a reason a lot of people become experienced in the sack, and normally, at least in part, it's because they enjoyed it and wanted more (yes, there are other reasons some people sleep around, but I'm talking probability).

So instead of holding it against someone who you think has been promiscuous, take it as a sign of a healthy appetite and enthusiasm. Or say your potential partner had a ton of sex with his or her ex; instead of being threatened by it, take stock in the fact both that they

logged the experience and had the passion to keep a sex life alive. Multiple years down the road, you'll want someone with that level of commitment and desire.

Desire-wise, sadly, it can't be denied that very little decent literature comes close to old randy Hank's books. Miller's most memorable novels are filled with examples of men and women who've got to have it, but for the tersest example—and of course the most extreme, as that's what Miller does—we can look to his passing praise in *Tropic of Cancer* of the Parisian prostitute named Germaine.

While other ladies of the French night would go about their business nonchalantly, Germaine "was different . . . she didn't rush things." Her secret, apparently, was having an excellent relationship with that part of her body that used to be called her "pudendum" (from the Latin word for shame!). Miller describes her spreading her legs wide apart as she "cupped it with her hands and stroked it some more, murmuring all the while that it was good, beautiful, a treasure, a little treasure. And it *was* good, that little pussy of hers!"

Germaine had figured out how to give herself pleasure, and in doing that, simultaneously learned how to give men pleasure. Being connected to your own body—regardless of your gender—is an enormous asset in being a good lover. You have come to understand what you like, at least in part, and, more important, you know *how* to like and that you *can* like. Just as someone who's eaten a lot of quality food has a better chance of becoming a chef, you know that sex can be good, so you want it more, try more, and it becomes better.

Germaine had figured out what sex could be and she wanted it: "A man! That was what she craved. A man with something between his legs that could tickle her, that could make her writhe in ecstasy, make her grab that bushy twat of hers with both hands and rub it joyfully, boastfully, proudly, with a sense of connection, a sense of life."

Through sex, she found access to life, and life became something she could transfer to the men she was with.

With that in mind, a civilian version of her history, i.e., a rather high "number" or a lot of wild experiences or whatever, starts becoming not something embarrassing or awful but in fact a gift—something you would want to share in. I think Miller hits the nail on the head when he says, "All the men she's been with and now you, just you, and barges going by, masts and hulls, the whole damned current of life flowing though you, through her, through all the guys behind you and after you, the flower and the birds and the sun streaming in."

So much for worrying about a person's past sexual life, right?

Now, I realize, of course, that a prostitute is the most extreme example, and don't get me wrong; I'm not suggesting you rush out to shack up with a professional, nor am I condoning unsafe sex practices or saying we should seek out potentially dangerous lovers. I'm simply saying that in less extreme cases, instead of holding someone's checkered past against him, we should take it as a good sign: that he's wired for pleasure and he sought that pleasure out. He's gone and had more fun, and he's going to give you more fun as a result.

To me this is all summed up rather nicely by the old Rodney Dangerfield joke about the guy who claimed that his wife gave the best blowjobs. The friend he's telling this to keeps pressing him, saying, "Really, they're that great?" and the guy keeps repeating something along the lines of, "Yes, yes, they're incredible." Finally, the friend stops and looks at him and says, "How do you think she got that good?" Word to the wise!

LADY'S CHATTERING LOVER

Ten Things Not to Say after Sex

ACCORDING TO JACK

Arm in arm, legs entwined, sweat beading on the marmoreal perfection of the human form, the dance of love just brought to its exquisite denouement, the Marlboro smoked, the snifter sipped dry, and now . . .

It's a dangerous time to speak. Post-amour, everyone is vulnerable, the defenses have been laid bare, and any utterance can be taken to have more meaning than intended. How many times have I said something I thought innocent—or even complimentary—only to have it heard by my beloved as something along the lines of "I wish you would turn into a pizza."

To see how this plays out in literature, we need only turn to one of the saucier of all highbrow novels, *Lady Chatterley's Lover*. There's enough sex in Lawrence's scandalous masterwork that I could find ten—yes, ten—things said after sex that you really wouldn't want to say today. Some are said by men, some are said by women, but both sexes should avoid pretty much all of them. So without further ado, and in the order in which they appear in the book, here they go:

I. Don't complain about the timing of someone's orgasm (or how they got there).

The quote in question: "You couldn't go off at the same time as a man, could you? You'd have to bring yourself off! You'd have to run the show."

Lady Chatterley's first lover, Michaelis, the colleague of her para-lyzed husband (who, admittedly, eventually encourages her to go get pregnant by someone else), is your basic well-dressed dandy. He visits the Chatterley home, he and the lady get busy, he finishes pretty quickly each time they get together, but the ladyship (as a good D. H. Lawrence heroine) keeps him inside of her and brings herself to an orgasm by rubbing herself on his thighs. So after a few times of this, apparently he's had enough and retorts with the above line.

Boys, the rule is never to talk about the woman's orgasm right after she's had it, much less criticize how she gets herself there (especially if you're a Señor Speedy!). Be thankful that she can come with you, by hook or by crook! Be even more thankful that even if you fall down on your job, she can handle matters herself! And whatever you do, don't make her self-conscious about it. You think you look great getting your business done? Even if you want to praise her (or yourself) for the success you just had, better keep still. Let it happen; don't shine light on it lest it disappear.

2. Never ask if your lover regrets the sex you just had.

The quote in question: "'You aren't sorry, are you?' he asked, as he went at her side."

The real lover of the title is the Chatterley manor gamekeeper, a peasant named Mellors. Mrs. Chatterley accidentally discovers him

washing himself by his hut and decides to get a piece o' dat. What follows is an intricate exploration of sex, psychology, and class relations (I was really impressed rereading the whole novel). And though Mellors, the classic strong, silent type, doesn't do too much yapping, his sensitive nature causes him to ask how the lady feels after their first tryst.

Asking if someone regrets the recently concluded festivities might sound nice on paper, but if the person is feeling sorry or uncomfortable after sex, she probably doesn't want to talk about it. It's either you or it's not you, but either way, you're not likely to be able to fix things. Let her brood; let her figure it out on her own. If she needs you, she'll ask you a question like, "Do you think that was a bad idea?" and then you can talk. Otherwise, zip it.

3. **Discussing your socioeconomic differences isn't sexy—or practical.**
The quote in question: "Good night, your Ladyship."

If you're the beneficiary of an other-side-of-the-tracks relationship, probably not such a good idea to point it out. When Mellors gets a little ticked off with Mrs. Chatterley for going away without promising to come back, this is his zinger of a good-bye. The better policy with a rich girl is to just appreciate the hosiery, the eau de parfum, the well-cared-for skin and leave it at that. And if you're the Julia Roberts pretty woman to his well-heeled Richard Gere, it's not in your interest to bring it up either. The more you mention the money discrepancy, the more power you give him to hold it against you.

4. **Do not allude, however vaguely, to your past lovers or experience.**
The quote in question: "We came off together that time . . . It's good when it's like that. Most folks live their lives through and they never know it."

When Mrs. Chatterley does eventually disprove Michaelis's jab and has a simultaneous orgasm with Mellors, the bohunk makes the mistake not only of mentioning it but of referring to other people's sex lives. Implication? He's had sex with other women! Uh-oh. What was just a very private moment with her feeling like she was special suddenly opens a window to his entire past, where she can feel like just the latest in a litany. No matter what observation you want to make about sex, keep everyone else out of it—no referring to your experience or your knowledge in general. Save such observations for less vulnerable moments.

5. Do not mention love to your no-strings-attached lover.
The quote in question: "I . . . I can't love you!"

Mrs. Chatterley has a breakdown after one of her sessions with the game master, confessing that she fears her heart will never be his (though soon it is). The problem is that she's forgetting that for him the whole affair is pretty much just a roll in the hay with a rich married woman. What Mrs. Chatterley doesn't realize is that most guys in most affairs would like as few strings attached as possible. If you think you're never going to fall in love with him, guess what: That's probably exactly what he'd prefer. No need to feel guilty or to say anything at all.

6. Post-coitus, don't *ever* ask if he or she loves you.
The quote in question: "You do love me, don't you?"

The classic "Don't ask!" question—because if you have to ask it, it probably isn't the case. Even worse, what response can the other person make? If he says he loves you, isn't that pretty much like having to ask for flowers, then seeing the roses on the tabletop and resenting that

you had to beg for them? And since the sentiment is unlikely to be real, you're almost insisting that he lie in his response to you, which, even to a person desperate for reassurance, has to be pretty cold comfort. This one is probably the worst all around; if you find it coming to your lips, you'd better keep quiet and start looking for real signs of love, not just hollow, forced assurances.

7. Never, under any circumstances, use the "c" word.
The quote in question: "Th'art good cunt, though, are'nt ter? Best bit o' cunt left on earth."

Though *Lady Chatterley's Lover* was written in the 1920s, the c-word already had a dodgy reputation (despite a variant of it being used in the Middle Ages by Chaucer). In this case, Mrs. Chatterley doesn't know what it means, but ultimately Mellors makes it clear that the word is pretty much what he likes about her. These days, that would be an utter disaster to say, but even then it wasn't great.

8. Tread with caution when talking about his penis.
The quote in question: "And now he's tiny and soft like a little bud of life!"

When a man's expired penis goes flaccid again, often tucking itself back into the scrotum like an undersized turtle head, he's not exactly proud of it. And "tiny," for the record, is never a word a guy wants to hear about his John Thomas. In the scene, you can also tell that Mrs. Chatterley is speaking to Mellors's unit in baby talk— also never a good thing. When a cock is high and mighty, *please* comment on it; when it's spent and downtrodden, don't make it into a stuffed animal.

9. Do not raise the issue of cohabitation out of the blue.

The quote in question: "I want to come and live with you always, soon."

While this might be a lovely sentiment to say in a real love relationship that had developed adequately, it's not the kind of idea you want to raise for the first time post-flagrante. And doing it with someone who isn't ready for cohabitation can only lead to disaster. In this case, Mrs. Chatterley already has a husband, and Mellors is used to living alone and in the woods. The last thing he'd want would be a bunkmate in his hut.

So if you picked your guy because he has that independent, bad-boy thing going on, it's likely to be a while before he wants to give that up and step into the ball and chain. He might abstractly suggest that he could spend the rest of his life with you, but if you reply that you're packing your hat boxes to move in, the good money says he'll start squirming.

10. Watch what you say about your lover's body.

The quote in question: "Tha's got the nicest arse of anybody. It's the nicest, nicest women's arse as is! An 'ivry bit of it is woman . . . Tha'rt not one o' them button-arsed lasses as should be lads . . . It's a bottom as could hold the world up, it is!"

Once again, Mellors's good intentions would have gotten him in quite the pickle these days. Men, if you're complimenting a woman's ass (or pretty much anything else), make sure you don't call her womanly, don't comment on its size, and don't under any circumstances contrast her—even favorably—to skinny girls. You might be trying to say that she looks like a *Playboy* centerfold; she's more likely to hear that she could never be in *Vogue*.

THE SUN ALSO RISES (BUT SOMETIMES NOT THE PENIS)

How to Handle Male "Issues"

ACCORDING TO JACK

It happens to the best of men: arousal but no lift, interest but no erection. When a man can't get or stay hard, the experience for him and his partner falls somewhere between awkward and utterly mortifying—I've even heard of men not calling women back because they were so ashamed of their inability to keep things on the up and up.

Most of you women out there will have known a guy to have had some, shall we say, "takeoff" issues in bed, and my guess is that most of you male readers will have had a little equipment trouble at one time or another as well. What's to be done?

In literature, there are quite a few famous examples of stage fright—perhaps Holden Caulfield's holdin' the prostitute at bay in *The Catcher in the Rye* is the most memorable—but for a more intricate treatment of how bound up virility is in the male ego and psyche, we have to turn to that most macho of macho writers, Ernest Hemingway.

My favorite line in his first novel, *The Sun Also Rises*, sets up the principle dichotomy in one of literature's greatest explorations of virility: "Nobody ever lives their life all the way up except bull-fighters." In Papa's world—or at least in the novel—it's bull-fighters vs. everyone else, the true men vs. the claimants, those who do vs. those who

watch (and write about it), and ultimately, those who can get it up vs. those who, in some form or another, stay slack.

What's fascinating about *The Sun Also Rises* is how it takes up the issue of erectile dysfunction (in this case permanent, though, as we will see, the lessons learned also apply to acute cases of nerves, drunk dick, second thoughts, and all the other ways of making the condor flightless) in the context of a book chock-full of all levels of stud-dom. Hemingway seems utterly obsessed with masculinity, as if he wanted *The Sun Also Rises* to be the definitive hierarchy of maleness, starting at wuss and moving all the way to bullfighter. In doing so he gives us the perfect backdrop to discuss the various issues involved in men not living up to their gender role—and shows us what women can do about it.

All these questions of performance and machismo are brought up by the central femme fatale, Lady Brett Ashley, former lover of the protagonist/narrator (and Hemingway stand-in), Jake Barnes.

Brett sets all the men in the novel atwitter. When we first meet her, Hemingway (Jake) describes her like this: "Brett was damned good-looking . . . She was built with curves like the hull of a racing yacht, and you missed none of it with that wool jersey."

We don't know yet about Brett and Jake's past; we don't know how he's her confidant and how she goes to him after each successive relationship of hers goes south. And we don't know yet about what seems to be the primary reason they're not together: her insatiable sexual appetite and his inability to gratify it, having received man's-worst-nightmare of a war wound.

Earlier Jake had had to explain his situation to a trollop he picked up in a café. When she cuddled and touched him he recoiled. That prompted the following exchange:

> *"What's the matter?"*
> *. . . "I got hurt in the war," he said.*
> *"Oh, that dirty war."*

Of course that makes you wonder why he let it go that far at all. (Why guys go through with things they aren't really interested in would be the subject of another chapter.) What's important to realize with dysfunction is that it's one thing when it's just a woman you've met on the street; it's another thing when it's someone like Brett, the woman you love, you've pined for, and whom you've watched flit about with all sorts of other men because you can't do the deed.

For Brett, the pain is equally acute. When she and Jake are on the street about to kiss, she stops him:

> "Don't touch me," she said. "Please don't touch me."
> "What's the matter?"
> "I can't stand it."
> "Oh, Brett."
> "You mustn't. You must know. I can't stand it, that's all.
> Oh, darling, please understand!"
> "Don't you love me?"
> "Love you? I simply turn all to jelly when you touch me."
> "Isn't there anything we can do about it?"

And that's the question: Isn't there anything we can do about it? In Jake's case, there really isn't, but as long as the parts are all still there and the man is genuinely willing, there are some things that can be done. Here are some pointers, based on the perils and pitfalls that Jake's situation makes clear.

1. Don't ask, "Is there anything we can do about it?"

Because men are so sensitive about sexual dysfunction, and because it creates about as embarrassing a moment as they can experience, the situation puts women in a really tough spot. Of course you just want to say, "Honey, is there something I can do to help?" But in some

cases, that's exactly what he *doesn't* want to hear. He's thinking, "No, I'm just dying from the pressure here, and the last thing I want you to do is even notice, much less try to do something!"

Even worse is if you say, "Is there something wrong?" or "Are you okay?" because, yes, there obviously is something wrong (you don't have to remind me!) and, no, I'm clearly not okay; I'm flaccid!

2. Don't make a big deal of it.

Jake describes being in the hospital and how an Italian colonel came to visit him and reacted to his plight (he had been fighting for the Italian army, as Hemingway himself did): "You, a foreigner . . . have given more than your life. . . . Che mala fortuna! Che mala fortuna!'"

Needless to say, Jake's situation is worse than your average guy just having a little trouble, but in any case, you don't want to treat it like the end of the world.

3. Don't take it personally.

At one point Jake says: "What happened to me is supposed to be funny. I never think about it," and Brett responds, "I laughed about it too, myself, once."

Laughing it off is actually the perfect solution, as long as it doesn't become chronic. Because here's the thing: You shouldn't take it personally. Trust me, a guy can have performance anxiety simply because he likes you a ton and is trying too hard to make you happy. Or he could have something else on his mind; some odd thing may have triggered his response; he may have had a lot to drink—any number of other things could be happening that have nothing to do with you or whether you're sexy. If it becomes a regular thing, there may be a more significant issue at work, but an isolated case or two—or jitters during the first few times you're together—is nothing to take as a bad sign.

4. Don't talk about it as it's happening.

Jake tells Brett, "Let's shut up about it" and then expresses his long aggravation, saying he was "pretty well through with the subject." Even if you have an impulse to bring it up while it's fresh, you're unlikely to tell the guy something he hasn't already thought (or is thinking). Jake says he had "considered it from most of its various angles," and if it's happened to your guy before, he probably has, too.

While it's going on, the guy's mind is running a thousand miles a minute, thinking through everything and punishing himself in every way possible. You want to derail this self-flagellation by not making it the focus of attention. If you need to talk about it later, wait till he's not lying there staring at his junk wanting to shoot it with a revolver. Trust me; the conversation will go better at a future date, for now he needs to get over his issue before he'll be ready to give you whatever reassurance you need.

5. Understand how much it upsets him.

After Brett has gone home, Jake lies in bed agonizing over his condition: "Of all the ways to be wounded. I suppose it was funny . . . Well, it was a rotten way to be wounded."

That sums things up pretty well—you'd want to be able to joke about it, but of course you can't. And unless you move into a cave and live the life of a hermit, life isn't likely to let you forget either. As Jake says, "Probably I never would have had any trouble if I hadn't run into Brett when they shipped me to England. I suppose she only wanted what she couldn't have. . . . The Catholic Church had an awfully good way of handling all that. Good advice, anyway. Not to think about it. . . . Try and take it sometime. I lay awake thinking and my mind jumping around. Then I couldn't keep away from it. . . . Then all of a sudden I started to cry."

This is pretty much the self-destructive thought process of a man who's letting his virility problem become a crisis of his entire identity.

So once you have a handle on *yourself* not taking it personally, help him realize that *he* shouldn't take it personally either. He probably thinks that he's stopped being a man in your eyes, so make sure he understands that you know it's a fluke and no big deal.

6. If it's chronic, either get help or get packing.

At one point, when Jake mentions his "accident" to a friend, the guy avoids discussion, saying "That's the sort of thing that can't be spoken of."

Unfortunately, men who have chronic conditions typically don't want to talk about it—ever—and can be very reluctant to go get help.

That's simply not acceptable from your side (or really from his, in the long run).

Brett at least has the wherewithal to tell Jake that if they tried to live together she would "just *tromper*" him—meaning lie to him—and run around "with everybody." She takes the blame herself, saying, "It's my fault, Jake. It's the way I'm made." But, really, it's how all of us are made. No one should think that she could live without sex forever, especially with a partner who, in the back of her mind, she will always suspect she failed to turn on. That will wear you down sooner or later, so make sure he gets help. If he's unwilling, that's all the proof you need that you have to go elsewhere.

Assuming, however, that it's not a long-term problem, what *can* a woman say or do when her man can't rev up the engines? There are a few possibilities—but know that any one of these can backfire, too, depending on the circumstances.

In order of most likely to go over well, here are five things you can say to help make the best of the situation:

1. **Don't worry, honey. It happens to all guys.**

 Granted, he might wonder how much experience you have, but at least he won't feel like he's the only loser on the planet. Misery sure does love company.

2. **We'll just touch for now—I love that.**

 This way he can feel like he's still giving you a decent experience, and it's possible that gentle, relaxed, not-trying-to-start-anything touching will eventually bring him around. I'd advise steering clear of his penis, though, at least until it starts showing life on its own. If you touch it, he might think you're trying again, and his guilt and feelings of failure can return and get in the way.

3. **You know what? It happens to me sometimes, too.**

 Guys might not realize that sometimes women don't get wet, even though they're aroused. Letting him know that it's a human thing, not just a flaw with his equipment, will help ease his mind.

4. **Why worry? I know you're a great lover. You make me happy all the time.**

 Clearly his confidence is not at an all-time high, so a little reassurance that he's not a disaster the rest of the time will boost his self-esteem. And right now, the thing he needs most is self-esteem.

5. **If there's something you'd like, just let me know.**

 Yes, this is pretty close to "Is there something I can do to help?" but the difference is in the approach. Asking what you can do implies there's a problem that needs fixing; asking if he wants something allows him to either articulate his needs or ignore your question. Still, this tactic is a bit risky, as he might feel as if you're disappointed with him. Sometimes, however, changing things up a little will put him in the right headspace and back on track. Just be careful when and how you ask.

Note that in all of these cases, the thing you need to make clear is that you're not mad at him, frustrated, or mocking him for not being able to get an erection (or for having lost one). You're fine with everything; you know there will be more chances, and you're not making a big deal of it.

Finally, keep in mind that men are a lot more complicated than they're given credit for. It might seem as if they're like light switches—easily turned on and only off when you turn them off—but there's a brain involved, and that can be a wild card. And when a man does have troubles, he really is at his most vulnerable. So be careful what you say and do. He's ultraexposed—in every way imaginable.

SABBATH'S PETER

How to Have Hot Sex at Any Age

ACCORDING TO MAURA

Until very recently, I worried my sex life would be over once I reached a certain age. Pressed to specify the exact number, I might've said forty-four, because my first and most important model of womanliness died when she was that old (and I was eight); I've always had a vague, superstitious notion that everything will end for me by that age, too. I've been told that I bear a striking resemblance to my mother, and I can see myself in old pictures of her: We have the same dark eyes, oval faces and pronounced chins; we have similarly lopsided smiles that create long crescents in our cheeks. So I can imagine what I'll look like at forty-four—but beyond that? I got nothing.

The other problem is that the industry I work in—magazine publishing—doesn't seem terribly interested in women past forty or so. As such, I've feared for years that my career would peter out around that time, and I would have to take a job making license plates. My old friends from the days when things were going relatively well would ditch me for being too drab and too broke, and between not having the psychological stability ensured by my social support network or enough money to keep myself looking good, the sex would dry up, as well.

My worst imaginings are fueled by America's youth-obsessed culture. (Which includes—I know, I know—those magazines I write for.) Here in the United States, women are constantly sent the message that in order to be sexually attractive, we should look as childlike as possible—with hairless pubic areas, unwrinkled skin, plump faces, and tiny bodies. While sexualized images of youthful nymphs are ubiquitous in our country, finding sexy representations of older goddesses is far more difficult. The "cougar" trend of recent years is helping somewhat, even if that seems to mean that older women who *look* twenty-five (but may be closer to twice that) are celebrated for their hotness. It's only fair to acknowledge, however, that the number of big-screen roles for women who are no longer of childbearing age but *are* admired for their sexiness is slowly increasing. (Up from an average annual rate of approximately zero.) Think of recent movies starring Diane Lane (born in 1965), Laura Linney (1964), and the smokin' French actress Isabelle Huppert (1953).

The cultural artifact that has given me the most hope that older folks can have perfectly active sex lives doesn't come from Hollywood or France, however. It comes from the great American writer Philip Roth by way of his conquest of a novel, *Sabbath's Theater*. In it, Roth writes with relish about the very busy sex life of a fifty-two-year-old woman, Drenka Balich. She effortlessly commands the sexual attention of a lot of men even though she hasn't had cosmetic surgery, isn't in terribly good shape, and often doesn't dress in flattering clothing. Roth conjures her with such gusto and vivacity that I came away from the book feeling confident, for the first time, that I might be able to keep getting laid well into my fifties, maybe even beyond. What's more, if Roth is to be believed, it's quite possible I'll actually be having the *best sex ever* then. Who knew?

Before I continue, let me acknowledge that I'm sure plenty of you think Roth's writing is offensive, sexist, at times even dangerously close to misogynistic. But come on—his novels can be such good,

naughty fun! His storytellers seduce *me*. They've had so much deliriously good sex with so many kinds of women, of so many ages, over the course of so many years, in so many novels, that I just can't write him off as an unremitting woman-hater. In fact, I often get the feeling that his narrators don't disdain women as much as they hate themselves for wanting so much sex. Still don't care for him? Fine; you can despise him as much as you want and even yet take something from his books. As critic Katie Roiphe said a few years ago in *The New York Times*, "One does not have to like Roth, or [his alter egos], to admire the intensely narrated spectacle of their sexual adventures."

Admire, yes. Or even "feel inspired by"—certainly if my reaction to *Sabbath's Theater* is any proof. Because while the sixty-four-year-old Mickey Sabbath of the title is pretty abhorrent (he is a physically repulsive adulterous husband), he helps to show how older women can be plenty tantalizing. Sabbath, narrating the novel in the third person, has had his share of improbably young lovers—and yet the lass who captures his heart is the aforementioned middle-aged woman, his mistress Drenka. No great beauty, she's pretty "in a rather efficient, businesslike way, except for her nose, a surprisingly bridgeless prizefighter's nose that created a sort of blur at the heart of her face." What makes her so captivating is her joie de vivre . . . or at least her joie de sex.

Sabbath, who has been forced into retirement by a sex scandal (so Rothian), is married to a recovered alcoholic, Roseanna. She puts up with him—and even supports him financially—because she fears that if she threw him out he'd commit suicide like her own father did. He stays in their chaste and joyless partnership in part because he needs the money—and since he's getting plenty of action from Drenka, life isn't so bad.

Drenka, a "less than startling-looking middle-aged woman corseted by all her smiling courtesy," is the doting mother of a local cop and the dutiful wife of a handsome innkeeper. Not above wearing

jeans and sweatshirts, she is "on the short side . . . a full, firmly made woman at the provocative edge of being just overweight, her shape, at her heaviest, reminiscent of those clay figurines molded circa 2000 B.C., fat little dolls with big breasts and big thighs . . ." The "soft fullness [of her breasts] had never ceased to captivate [Sabbath]. It was supposed to be otherwise, with the musculature everywhere losing its firmness, but even where her skin had gone papery at the low point of her neckline, even that palm-size diamond of minutely crosshatched flesh intensified not merely her enduring allure but his tender feeling for her as well."

Can any of Roth's detractors read that last sentence without at least *suspecting* that he is no unremitting misogynist? He takes a microscopic lens to the aging female body and finds it defiantly, resoundingly, *hot*. That Sabbath is a lecherous curmudgeon who is still very in touch, shall we say, with his fondness for nubile bodies makes his affection for Drenka in the face of her visible decay all the more touching. (Roth himself told one interviewer, "Passion doesn't change, but you change—you become older. The thirst for women becomes more poignant. And there is a power in the pathos of sex it didn't have before." Um, Mr. Roth, would you happen to be free tonight? For, you know, a little writerly guidance?)

Wondering what makes Drenka such a sexual cynosure? As I'm sure you've noticed, she doesn't look anything like Samantha Jones of *Sex and the City* fame. And yet they're very similar in the sense that they both like sex quite a lot and have no hang-ups about having it. Lots of it. Drenka, like Samantha, is someone who gives free play to "the force that wants more and more." She's a sexual hedonist. And by "more and more," what Roth means is an absurd amount of sex with an unreal number of men.

Drenka is, in most respects, a mostly "realistic" character, but the outrageous number of studs she schtups—all of whom care about and respect her—strains the imagination a bit. (Her loving husband

is hot for her, too, incidentally, but she doesn't enjoy their sex; she goes along with it out of her sense of loyalty to him.) But it's not the *quantity* of paramours that makes Drenka admirable. What we should be paying attention to is her life force, as expressed through her sexual insatiability. Drenka wants to have sex because she wants pleasure and experience; she craves human connection. Her lust for lust makes her a force to be reckoned with. Knowing what she wants and being unafraid to go after it make her deeply confident. She's completely at ease with herself and her sexuality. She is, without shame or embarrassment, "a conventional woman who would do anything." (Anything . . . including having phone sex with other men while jerking Sabbath off. Or doing it with a twenty-year-old lesbian as Sabbath looks on.) As those who would accuse Roth of misogyny should note, he glorifies a female character who revels in her sexuality—the type whom many people would call a slut—rather than maligning or caricaturing her.

Before you go jumping to the wrong conclusion, I should say that Drenka isn't fucking so much because she's so fucked up, as Roth is careful to point out. She was raised with affection by loving parents—in contrast to Sabbath's wife, Roseanna, who's so neurotic that she's deeply undesirable, if also (or concomitantly) pitiful. By conventional standards, childless Roseanna is the more attractive one; she's slim, boyishly pretty, and significantly younger than Drenka. But it's matronly Drenka who has everyone going gaga. She's not only maternally shaped but maternally minded: warm and loving. In fact, sometimes, when Sabbath is with her, he is "pierced by the sharpest of longings for his late little mother."

Do I admire Drenka's lascivious behavior in its specifics? Not quite. Would *I* ever feel comfortable having multiple simultaneous lovers? I don't think so. Am I urging you on to get out there and have tons of casual sex? Absolutely not! What I want to emphasize is the creativity, enthusiasm, and abandon Drenka brings to her sex life,

and her blissful disregard for societal standards. Drenka isn't worried about how our culture seems to think that women over forty barely have sex lives; she's not a bit anxious about the fact that she doesn't look anything like a cover model. Drenka shows us that it's possible to be a sex object at her age—and that the best way to be a sex object at *any* age is to be comfortable in your own skin, no matter how wrinkled, papery, or loose it might be.

Though I'm pretty sure adultery isn't necessary to keep things interesting as we get older, encouraging and exploring our desires seems crucial, especially when we no longer look anything like the poster children for pop culture's libidinous fantasies. Making an effort to be imaginative and adventurous becomes increasingly important as the years pass. (Simply experimenting with a vibrator, if you've never tried it before, will certainly add years, if not decades, to your coital span.) Much as "going beyond your comfort zone" is a hackneyed phrase, there's something to it. I'm frequently delighted by how much I find myself liking things I thought I hated—Antonioni's early films, Rothko's paintings, brussels sprouts, and oh boy, Earl Grey tea. Similarly, certain activities that I hated with one boyfriend can be surprisingly satisfying with another.

Had I come across Drenka when I was very younger and more prudish, I might not have liked her very much, either. But now I'm wise enough to be glad to know her, if only in the fictional sense, and not the biblical.

Jack says:

Give me a D; give me an R, an E, N, K, A! Have sex early; have sex late. Who do we appreciate? Dren-KA!

Yes, as I write at greater length in the Tropic of Romancer

chapter, women (and men) who are really into it can make sex *much* better for the other person. Now, we do have to wonder a bit how much Drenka is just the wish fulfillment of Roth's imagination, but even so, you're totally right in thinking that being a little like her would go a long way. (Imagine if Jane Eyre had had a little Drenka blood in her—the novel sure would have turned out differently!)

So, yes, on behalf of all men, I encourage all you women to be enthusiasts. You'll make us happy and give us that much more reason to try to make you happy back. I can't guarantee it will be enough, but it definitely can't hurt, and hopefully you'll have a little fun in the process.

MIDSUMMER'S (OR ANY OTHER SEASON'S) NIGHTMARE

Signs You Should Abandon Ship

Chapter 22

MOBY DICKHEADS

Why Workaholics and Other Obsessives Are Bad News

ACCORDING TO MAURA

Perhaps you are drawn—like I have been for most of my life—to men with big ambitions and even bigger work ethics: not-enough-hours-in-the-day types who are single-mindedly focused on some creative or entrepreneurial endeavor. Maybe he's a young med school student or an aspiring lawyer striving to graduate at the top of his class. Maybe he's working on an epic first novel inspired by the Amanda Knox story, or a conceptual art project that involves turning trash into mammoth garbage sculptures. Maybe he's founding a non-profit that will improve health practices in developing countries, or he has the more down-to-earth goal of simply hoping to make a few million within the next five years through the hedge fund he and some b-school buddies started up. Whatever it is, you really believe he's going to pull it off—it's been nothing but green lights all his life and his future seems so bright that you wear your Ray-Bans in his presence.

Yet . . . though you've been dating exclusively for a while now, you haven't progressed much in terms of intimacy. You're still at the dinner-and-sex-on-Saturdays level; he's sorry but he just doesn't have time for anything more. If he does manage to make time for you on

one additional weeknight, he's on his iPhone through more than half the meal, or the two of you order takeout because he's too exhausted to deal with a restaurant. Afterward, he musters the strength for intercourse (he wouldn't want to miss out on *that*), but forget about the spooning; he passes out and begins snoring immediately. You finally drift off to sleep yourself, only to be roused at five a.m. by that Jay-Z ringtone of his . . . which is starting to get on your nerves. By the time you get out of bed, he's gone.

You were cool with the slow pace at first, because, hey, you're an independent person yourself; you didn't want to rush into anything either. But by this point, you're understandably impatient. So you tell Mr. Overachiever you'd like to be able to count on seeing him a little more often. He informs you—in a perfectly nice and even affectionate way—that he's already giving you all the scanty free time he has.

You start to wonder if "single-minded" is the opposite of "relationship-minded." I'm here to tell you it *is*.

Please do not stick it out to see how things might change when— and if—he achieves his goal. Because during that waiting period, you'll suffer through chronic disappointment and get so used to substandard treatment that it will affect the way you approach subsequent relationships. Besides, if you do bide your time, there are no guarantees about what he'll do once he manages to get to the top of the mountain he's been climbing for so long. Chances are very good he'll notice there's a bigger rock to climb, over yonder, at which point the cycle will begin all over again. A workaholic is not going to stop being a workaholic simply because he meets someone as lovely as you or achieves whatever his immediate objective is. Workaholism is a way of life—an attempt to impose order on the chaos of existence— even more than a means to a specific end. Workaholics can change their habits gradually, but they're usually not moved to do that unless something extreme happens—like a serious injury, the death of someone significant, or a midlife crisis. On the other hand, plenty of

workaholics respond to life-changing experiences by working harder than ever—as does Captain Ahab, the compelling seaman at the center of Herman Melville's classic, *Moby-Dick*.

That endearing, enduring book tells of the final, fateful voyage of the *Pequod*, a whale ship commanded by Ahab—a man obsessed with whaling in general who becomes fixated on hunting a certain white giant in particular. Ahab is another literary orphan: Left parentless when his widowed mother died twelve months after giving birth to him, he had little choice but to begin working at a very young age. As he laments in a soul-wrenching discussion with his first mate, Starbuck, Ahab "struck" his first whale when he was just an eighteen-year-old "boy-harpooner." Since then, as he goes on to say, his life has been: "Forty years of continual whaling! Forty years of privation, and peril, and storm-time! Forty years on the pitiless sea! For forty years has Ahab [who sometimes talks about himself in the third person] forsaken the peaceful land, for forty years to make war on the horrors of the deep!"

Three voyages prior to the *Pequod*'s last waltz, Ahab, nearing his sixtieth birthday, got married for the first time in his life to a "sweet, resigned girl." But he was too busy to enjoy a proper honeymoon: He "sailed for Cape Horn the next day" after their ceremony. As he admits, he has spent the entire marriage "whole oceans away, from that young girl-wife I wedded"—and worlds away from their child, too. If you ask me, Ahab throws himself into work in part because it distracts him—as it distracts so many of us—from the difficult, metaphysical questions he would have to face if he had more time to reflect on them. Like alcoholics, who drink to escape their dark emotions, workaholics work in the hopes of achieving a certain kind of immortality that will help them stave off concerns about death and the meaning of life; they strive to make some mark on the world, to leave something lasting behind—if only fortunes for their families. And yet, ironically, workaholism makes it all the more difficult to find

a relationship that could help alleviate their existential despair in a more profound way.

(Incidentally, Ahab serves as a counterpoint to the main character in what is probably Melville's second most-famous story, *Bartleby the Scrivener*. Apparently, he wrote that laugh-out-loud-funny novella in response to the terrible reception of *Moby-Dick*—panned by critics, largely ignored by the public for years—and the ennui and despondency it caused him. Not unlike Ahab, who lives in his ship, Bartleby lives in the law firm where he works as a copier. He sleeps on the floor under his desk. In contrast to Melville's better-known character, though, Bartleby hates to work; whenever he's asked to do just about *anything*, his answer is "I would prefer not to"—until he reaches a point where he's doing nothing all day long. One could argue that both Ahab and Bartleby are responding to the absurdity of life in opposing ways: One is making an enormous effort to wrest some control over it, and the other is refusing to participate in it as much as possible.)

After slaving away for so long, Ahab himself is starting to get a little sick of the relentless schedule he keeps. He laments "the desolation of solitude" his life has been, and the "cruel, remorseless emperor [who] commands [him] . . . against all natural loving and longings . . . recklessly making [him] do what in [his] own proper, natural heart, I durst not so much as dare." (That unfeeling dictator he refers to is his own psyche.) But, though Ahab can acknowledge—and even question—his monomaniacal behavior, he can't bring himself to stop. In fact, at the moment we meet him, it's more crucial than ever that he bust his tail. Because he wants to bust a very specific whale: an outsized albinic white nicknamed Moby-Dick. Ahab is driven by a lust for vengeance: During a voyage he took prior to the novel's opening, Moby destroyed Ahab's ship and bit off his leg. And you better believe Ahab is going to work, work, work—and whale, whale, whale—till he gets payback.

As Eudora Welty put it in her collection of essays *On Writing*,

Moby-Dick's "task as a symbol was so big . . . that he had to be a whale." Which is to say that Moby has metaphoric significance on many levels. For starters, he can be seen as a personification (or whale-ification?) of cruel fate, of some kind of god, of a life-defining goal, of Ahab's tormented soul (which has also handicapped him, psychologically and emotionally, so that he is constantly struggling to overcome it). He can be seen as the desire for revenge made incarnate—and as a representation of how elusive a sense of accomplishment can be for Ahab and his ilk; the thing they're after keeps swimming away from them, always just out of reach. Moby-Dick really *is* enormous.

Yet if anyone is capable of hunting him down, it's Ahab. He is, without a doubt, a serious bad-ass—a man of great physical and psychological courage. But no matter how much there is to admire about him, *I would never seriously date a guy like that,* let alone get hitched to him. Because as Ahab admits to Starbuck, he's never really been a spouse to his wife. Rather, he made her "a widow with her husband alive! . . . Aye, I widowed that poor girl when I married her." By spending so much time away from home, he is nearly as good as dead to her, in other words. And though we don't get any direct insight into how she feels about being home alone all the time, my guess is that she's pretty miserable—as any of us would be if the person we were married to was constantly out at sea, literally or metaphorically.

Dear readers, Melville's classic is a cautionary tale that operates on as many levels as the whale symbol does, warning us—among other things—that a relationship in which you're yearning for closeness and pining for face time more often than you're getting it is rarely worth it. (Particularly if it starts out that way, and there's no indication it'll change any time soon.) Don't let what happened to Mrs. Ahab happen to you. Don't lose your life to a person who has dedicated *his* life to work. Forego the Moby Dickheads! Let *them* go down with the ship—and save yourself while you still can.

There are plenty of other harpooners in the sea.

Chapter 23

THE BRIEF WONDROUS LIFE
OF MY LAST RELATIONSHIP

Are Men Genetically Coded to Cheat?

ACCORDING TO JACK

Men cheat—we can't help ourselves, right? We're pretty much still just Homo erectus, following our biological imperative to chase any skirt possible. So goes the conventional logic, but to me that's an absurd cop-out.

Even if it's true, as sociobiologists claim, that when men were still wearing pelts, there were no relationships and the survival of the species depended on us impregnating as many hominid females as we could, what of it? In the same way that today I choose to grill my buffalo burger rather than eat it raw—and enjoy it a hell of a lot more that way—can't cultured man simply not give in to his prehistoric impulses? Haven't we evolved to the point where sex can—and should—be a lot more than just the delivery of the genetic matter?

Don't get me wrong: I'm aware that being monogamous is a lot more challenging than lighting a charcoal grill. And I confess to having the stereotypical-male, skin-level desire: my eyes see, sometimes my insides shudder, and a few times a day some part of me can't help wonder what it would be like to sleep with this woman or that. We all know that most men are like this, but the civilized among us make themselves as immune as possible.

The tougher thing to describe is the psychology of identity behind men's desire to seduce. In my own case, it took me a long time to realize how much attention I need as a person and that, despite all the confidence I have and successes I've had in various quadrants of my life, a lot of me still just wants to be reassured that I'm liked. As men we're taught to be independent and self-sufficient, but few of us are, can, or even should be.

We need others for all kinds of reasons, and we like to be needed by them as well. Seduction—for both men and women—gives us the sense that someone wants us, that she endorses us and will let us influence her. We know that men often try to seduce women for the same reasons they try to make money—for power and prestige—but when you look deeper, you see that it's more than just belt-notching. Sex and seduction help us believe in ourselves, to become ourselves even, and that can be a tough thing to give up.

And, sadly, though we want to become ourselves as men, we rarely realize how much it's not other *people*, but a single *person* who can help do that. Many, perhaps most of us, dream of spending our lives with a partner, having all the comfort, intimacy, trust, and history that one can gather only by getting together with someone and staying together. But what's not on that list of benefits is "self"—and that's the key to it all. We think we get selfhood by influencing and seducing, doing and building and earning, but a lot of men never experience the deeper, more meaningful self that can be achieved in the sharing and communing, in all the trials and triumphs, with a lifelong partner.

This is all summed up rather nicely by the cheating but otherwise utterly delightful narrator of *The Brief Wondrous Life of Oscar Wao*—Yunior de Las Casas, Dominican player extraordinaire and on-and-off lover of Oscar's sister, Lola.

Yunior knows he's a cheater, knows he has an irrepressible need to seduce. Describing how he's steadily juggling three women (plus picking up others on the side), he explains, "A heart like mine, which

never got any kind of affection growing up, is terrible above all things."

Terrible, perhaps—certainly so for the person cheated on. But Yunior's confession also points to the pitiable element behind a lot of human straying: We need affection, we've always needed affection, and a deficit from one phase of our lives can carry over into the next.

The irony, of course, is that the cheater might very well have access to that affection from someone who loves him—and yet it's not enough. That was certainly true for Yunior, who was not only loved by Lola but also loved (and esteemed) her inordinately. Late in the book when he summarizes why he and Lola didn't end up together, he says simply, "Couldn't keep my rabo in my pants even though she was the most beautiful fucking girl in the world." Lola is described as being extremely intelligent, president of her sorority, and a track star with world-class legs and *culo*—why wasn't she enough?

Because, as anyone who has ever been cheated on should know, it's often not about you at all. The unfaithful person has needs of his own to fulfill, and even if you're capable of fulfilling them, he might be incapable of getting it from you. (Though, yes, if you've been denying your partner sex for a long time or if it's gotten so routine that both parties are just going through the motions, then infidelity is a sad but not unusual result.)

For Yunior, however, it's as if it's a foregone conclusion that he's going to cheat. At a certain point he says he's a "sucio" (a dirty guy) and at another that he loves cheating as much as the Oscar of the title loves writing.

It's sad, really, because if you're in a relationship and yet find yourself wanting to act on the unfaithful messages your nether regions are sending, it's time for some heavy-duty examination—of your relationship and of yourself.

Self should come first, asking the question of what's really going on. Is the new person just attractive and you feel the twitch? If so,

remember that your fantasy might well be better than the realization would be. Or has it been a long time since you've been with someone new? Okay, that might be tough, but why? Maybe it means the sex in your relationship has gone stagnant. (Is that your fault? Your partner's? Is it laziness or are there deeper problems? All this should be explored.) If that's the case, you're perhaps just missing the physical pleasure, and you should try to resurrect your love life with your current partner first.

But maybe your sex life *is* fine with your partner, but you're missing the seduction thrill. That means you're still using seduction to bolster your ego, and clearly your sense of self isn't as confident and secure as it needs to be. And here, too, you have to ask if you are not doing enough or if your partner is not doing what you need—or both. Feeling the need to seduce should be a wake-up call that you're not getting the ego satisfaction that's necessary from the other areas of your life. You should probably try to work on those before you go and cheat on the partner you love.

Or perhaps the relationship itself is the culprit: You're not having sex because your partner doesn't want to or you don't want to, and you want to cheat because he or she's not making you feel how you need to feel.

But realize this: Infidelity is a symptom, not a solution. Ultimately the impulse to cheat might help you get out of a bad relationship, but first you need to see if the relationship is worth trying to hold on to. Striving for monogamy helps you get the most out of a partnership by facing the challenges head-on—the only way it works.

It's clear that none of these questions is about the supposed object of the cheating desire; they're about you and your relationship and how those things are doing. (And if you're asking yourself if the new person would be "better for you" than the person you're with, remember that you probably barely know her or him, are thinking wishfully, and eventually that individual will have their tics and foibles and annoyances just as your current partner does.)

For a lot of us, it's daunting to think that we might have sex with only one person for the rest of our lives, but at the same time, maybe it just requires a rethinking of what sex means. The key to long-term sexual happiness is to have sex be less about seduction, ego, and the symbolic sense of power and more about pleasure, feeling, and expression of intimacy. With that model, the best sex is sex with someone you know and love, and it should get better and better. I understand that there are only so many ways of having sex and you might sometimes feel in a rut, but, truthfully, that's just a challenge to expand your habits, leave your comfort zones, and grow as a person with your partner. Every challenge to having a fuller sex life with someone you love makes you a better person—more creative, expressive, and self-aware. Sex with only one person is the hard way, but it's the way that makes us grow and develop to be the fullest people we can be.

Yunior wasn't ready to go there and instead continued his tomcat ways until Lola finally dumped him for good and married someone else. It's clear that he always loved her best but wasn't able to do the hard work to fix himself. As he puts it: "I should have checked myself into Bootie-Rehab. But if you thought I was going to do that, you don't know Dominican men."

The rest of us should learn from his example. Most impulses toward infidelity are ultimately either passing physical blips or signs that something else is wrong. If you go after the problems themselves, then the Band-Aid solution of cheating stops being worth it. So instead of letting a wandering eye turn into an elicit romp, fix the problem at its source. You'll have the reward of that much richer a relationship, a self, or both.

Maura says:

Not so long ago, I put the very question Jack takes up here to the man I'm dating: Are human males biologically programmed to cheat? This was his answer: "I do want to sleep with somewhere between five and ten percent of the women I come across. But as an evolved human being, I'm able to control that desire—and I choose not to give in to it because what I want more than sex with those random people is my relationship with you, and the trust we have. I know you'd be hurt and dump me in a second if I slept with someone else, so being faithful is easy."

Chapter 24

REVOLUTIONARY ROAD
TO HELL

Lose That Guy Who Is Still Trying to Find Himself

ACCORDING TO MAURA

In my midtwenties, I thought I was in love. The man in question found New York City as magical as I did, and we were always off on some little adventure—discovering the secret garden behind a West Village church; voyaging to some far-flung dive to find the crooner who sings Sinatra songs with a Tom Waits voice; or happening upon that gritty gem of a restaurant near CBGB and getting the seats on the side of the bar so we could have a full view of the kitchen performance. We wanted to capture the unexpected splendor of those scenes in words; we dreamed of becoming writers.

He'd recently quit a big-money job in corporate finance. Movies were his true passion, and he wanted to be a screenwriter like the great American dramatist William Goldman—the guy who wrote *Butch Cassidy and the Sundance Kid*, *The Princess Bride*, and *All the President's Men*. But having good taste in movies, which he did, is one thing; being able to come up with the narratives that propel them is another.

Now, just about everyone who wants to make it big as a writer—of movies or novels—has to struggle for a good long time before they make it; often they must sacrifice well-paying jobs and more stable careers and go through a period of poverty, strife, uncertainty, doubt,

and deprivation. They have to face repeated rejections and setbacks and muster the psychological fortitude to soldier through them. But although this guy wanted the fame and recognition that would come of being a Goldman, he wasn't willing to take the necessary risks. Instead, he played it safe. After doing a few months of soul searching, he decided he wanted to go to business school.

Now, there's not necessarily anything wrong with that, but it's a funny choice for a person who'd been looking for a more artistic way to earn a living; for a person who thought, as he did, that he was fated to live an exceptional life of film, fame, and fortune.

Follow the money: It was, perhaps, William Goldman's most famous line; it also sums up what my dude had decided to do.

I ran into this person a few years ago, near Park Avenue, as I was walking to the subway after dinner with a *Marie Claire* editor. It seemed like you could reach behind his ear and miraculously draw a one-hundred-dollar bill; you looked at him and you saw the wealth— the perfectly tailored suit, the shiny tie, the gleaming Italian leather on his feet, the expensive hairstyle. What a coincidence, to see each other! I was curious about how his life had turned out, so we bopped into a nearby bar for a drink. To my great surprise, I didn't find him anywhere near as smart or unusual as he used to seem; in fact, he was rather dull—and absurdly arrogant in a way that many people who make easy money seem to be. He described the vacation home he'd recently purchased; he told me about the work he was doing; he said he and his wife had recently had a baby; and he mentioned that he'd thought many times, through the years, about fucking me. (Yes, he used the "F" word.)

If I'd done almost anything but what I'd done, I have the feeling he would've suggested we go back to the hotel where he was staying. But I didn't want to do that to his wife; even more, I didn't want to do it to myself. So I looked away and said, "Tell me more about that new baby girl!"

He reminded me quite a bit of Frank Wheeler—the fictional pro-
tagonist at the bitter heart of Richard Yates's sardonic masterpiece,
Revolutionary Road. Wheeler, a Columbia University graduate, begins
coming into his own in his early twenties. During that period, for
"the first time in his life . . . he was admired, and the fact that girls
could actually want to go to bed with him was only slightly more
remarkable than his other concurrent discovery—that men . . . could
actually want to listen to him. . . . All he would ever need . . . was the
time and freedom to find himself . . . [He] hardly ever entertained a
doubt of his own exceptional merit."

A charismatic man—just smart enough to be a danger to him-
self—Frank marries a beautiful young aspiring actress, April. (In the
movie version, Frank is played by Leonardo DiCaprio; April, by Kate
Winslet.) When she gets pregnant before they're ready to be parents,
April would like to induce a miscarriage. But Frank thinks that's crazy
talk—and less out of a sense that it's the moral thing to do and more
because it's the *normal* thing to do, he decides to take a boring but
well-paying job. They eventually have a second child "to prove that
the first one hadn't been a mistake" and buy a house in the Connecti-
cut 'burbs to keep up with the Joneses.

Frank is dissatisfied by the life he's built for himself. He thinks his
corporate nine-to-five gig is "the dullest job you can possibly imag-
ine." He's not particularly fond of his kids—who are in grade school
in 1955, the year the book begins. He condescends to his neighbors.
He sees April as "the graceless, suffering creature whose existence he
tried every day of his life to deny." To make matters even shabbier, he
carries on an affair with a vulnerable secretary who works in his office.
And yet, despite the mess he's making, he continues to believe he's
meant for better things.

Paradoxically, Frank's very disdain for his life helps to console
him; he is diligent about figuring out ways to firm up his conviction
that he's smarter and more interesting than the bland suburbanites

and office drones he's surrounded by. Indeed, his one keenly developed talent is his remarkable ability to articulate what's wrong with everyone else in America—though he's a master at overlooking truths about himself. One evening, over drinks with his wife and their "friends," he complains, "Nobody thinks or feels or cares any more . . . [or] believes in anything except their own comfortable little God damn mediocrity. "

The better Frank gets at living a cushy, conventional life while telling himself he's unusual, the more painful April finds his hypocritical smugness. She never *could* act very well—not on the stage or in the private setting of her bedroom—and along the same lines, she's never been able to fool herself the way Frank can. She is slowly being suffocated by her marriage. Her husband complains about how stultifying conformity is—but at the same time, he becomes more similar to the people he looks down on with every major life choice he makes. April, on the other hand, begins trying to rebel. She's not a terribly likable character, but as I read the book a second time, I saw that she was more truthful than her husband—courageous enough to take an honest look at her life, and a few big risks.

Having harbored a lifelong dream of becoming a thespian, April goes out for community theater and is cast in the lead female role. Her performance on the big night is a disaster, however—and she knows it. But having tried and failed, she's learned a valuable lesson: Acting is no way out of her dissatisfaction. Her next idea would transform their life more dramatically than any theatrical turn: She suggests they all move to Paris, where she'd find work as a NATO secretary, thereby giving Frank the time, finally, to find himself. It's a surprising suggestion, all the more so because it was unusual for a woman like April—a young affluent 1950s mother—to work a day job, never mind being the sole breadwinner. But April doesn't care about "conventional morality," the way Frank does; she just wants to be less miserable.

Very reluctantly—perhaps somewhat aware that if he looks for himself, he won't find much—Frank agrees to go to Paris. But when his bosses suddenly offer him a big promotion, and April almost simultaneously discovers she's pregnant, Frank seizes the chance to back out of the trip. Though he's not terribly interested in the new job and doesn't really want another kid, being able to postpone facing up to his mediocrity suits him just fine.

Shortly after Frank reneges on the European sojourn, April gives herself a DIY abortion, knowing that it will wreck her marriage—and maybe worse.

Of course, plenty of people are happier deceiving themselves than they would be forcing themselves to recognize their own shortcomings, limitations, and personal failings. But those of us like April, who are striving to be true to ourselves because we believe that it's the only way to really find contentment, are going to suffer if we couple up with people as practiced in the art of self-deception as Frank.

Luckily today, much more so than in April's time, divorce is an option for women who feel trapped in unhappy marriages; so is a career. (As for safe abortions, well, at the rate we're going, they may soon be just as unavailable in the future as they were in the '50s.) But all the options we have today mean we *really* shouldn't slide into a relationship full of small lies with a person who refuses to see himself for what he is.

Plenty of people are like Frank—they'd rather take the easy route every time a life decision needs to be made, rather than do any meaningful soul-searching. But the unfounded self-importance and egotism of such folks can become infuriating, especially for spouses who are stuck with them forever. What's more, someone who can't look truthfully at his own life often becomes a master of all kinds of dishonesty; it's no coincidence that Frank's kind are often cheaters, too. The best relationships—the kind we should be aiming for—involve people we can both believe in, and believe. The Franks of the world

are unpleasant spouses not *because* they're conventional, but because they've dishonestly built their egos around the idea that they're *uncon*ventional—exceptional, interesting, especially smart.

It may sound funny to say this, but a person who has gone after his dreams, even if only to fail and move on, is going to be a more loving partner—though probably not a more wealthy partner—than someone who's always coasted by on his natural talents without ever quite living up to his promise or testing his abilities. Someone who has tried is likely to know himself, to be humble, and to have empathy. He doesn't tell himself he's superior to everyone around him. He doesn't look at his job or the woman in his life and think, "Eh, I could do better." Rather, if he's dissatisfied, he's more likely to think about constructive ways to make things better. The Franks, conversely, refuse to see how much like everyone else they are. They lack the humility we all need to truly love another human being (and ourselves).

To distinguish yourself in modern-day America, like Frank once thought he could, you need more than big ideas, intelligence, and talent. (More, too, than a hookup with a reality TV show producer.) What's just as important is the courage to separate from the crowd in your habits, thoughts, and actions. Having a supportive partner who urges you on—and promises to stand by you as you muddle through—helps immeasurably; in fact, it's a dream in itself. Frank never understood that. Don't make his mistake.

SONS AND MOTHER-LOVERS

Yes, He Can Love His Mom Too Much

ACCORDING TO MAURA

W hen it comes to straightforward signs that an eligible bachelor will make a good mate—he is kind to animals, loyal to his friends, polite to waiters, taxi drivers, and toll-booth operators—can anything trump a healthy relationship with his mother? A man who feels deep respect and fondness for his mama is likely to be capable of real intimacy and abiding love; chances are good that he'll treat his lady partner with reverence and adoration, too. As my friend's mother, Mary Catherine, a psychotherapist, put it: "Men who've had very positive relationships with their mothers often have similarly positive attitudes toward women in general; they're trusting, respectful, and very comfortable around them." Much harder to be with are men whose mothers were neglectful, difficult, or unavailable—due to depression, for instance, or aloof personalities. "These men are difficult and confusing, because they feel needy, mistrustful, and uncertain, all at once," according to Mary Catherine.

All this said, some men can be a little *too* close to their moms, admiring them so intensely and identifying with them so strongly that they have trouble advancing beyond the maternal bond; they just can't seem to find a woman who measures up. Often this happens if a

mother is single or unhappily married—and her son becomes something of a stand-in for a good husband. Other times, the connection between the two is ratcheted up by a major emotional catalyst—like the death of another child or a period of extended convalescence for the boy. Frequently, the matriarchs in such duos—the Jocastas, if you will—are complicit, if subconsciously: They become so emotionally reliant on their son's affection and confidence that they encourage the boys to remain psychologically tethered.

A prime example: Paul Morel, the young painter at the center of D. H. Lawrence's *Sons and Lovers*. The novel is, among other things, one long exhortation to be wary of men who consider their mothers their closest confidantes. Set in Nottinghamshire, England, a coal-mining town, at the turn of the century, it revolves around the relationship between Paul and his mother, a feminist born before her time. She is a woman with a "curious, receptive mind . . . [who] loved ideas . . . [and a good] argument on religion or philosophy or politics with some educated man." And yet, despite her intellectual bent, she marries an uneducated miner because of the intense physical connection they have. Their sex is great, but Morel père is a disappointment to her in all other ways—he drinks too much, he's bad with money, and, worst of all, she just can't have an interesting conversation with him. To console herself, Mrs. Morel devotes herself completely to her children and ends up feeling the most intense bonds of her life with them—in particular with her second child, Paul. When he's born, she holds him in her arms, thinks about how she doesn't love her husband, and feels "as if the navel string that had connected [Paul's] frail little body with hers had not been broken. A wave of hot love went over her."

That's one uncomfortably sexual sentence, as I may not have to tell you.

As Paul—more sensitive and perceptive than his siblings—goes from baby to adult, he begins to feel reciprocal passion for his

mother. Starting in his boyhood, her moods predict his own: "When she fretted he understood, and could have no peace," Lawrence writes. "His soul seemed always attentive to her." Instead of pulling away from his mother during adolescence, as so many children do, he only gets closer to her. After landing his first job at age fourteen, clerking at a factory that manufactures surgical supplies, Paul encourages her to live vicariously by telling her the stories of his days, "like an Arabian Nights." When her other favorite, Paul's older brother, William, leaves home for a gig in London, Paul and she are bound ever closer. Lawrence describes it this way: "Mrs. Morel clung now to Paul . . . and he still stuck to his mother. Everything he did was for her. She waited for his coming home in the evening, and then she unburdened herself of all she had pondered, or of all that had occurred to her during the day. He sat and listened with his earnestness. The two shared lives." As if all that weren't eyebrow-raising enough, he also blatantly *flirts* with her, telling her how attractive she is and picking forget-me-nots for her. Rather than discouraging this behavior, she delights in it.

Before Paul is old enough to move out of the house, William dies due to complications from pneumonia—and the oedipal screws tighten, especially after Paul's mother becomes jealous of his burgeoning relationship with a neighbor girl named Miriam. Telling herself *Miriam* is too possessive, Mrs. Morel decides she has to "fight to keep Paul." And, whoa, does she. One night, after Paul gets so distracted during a visit from Miriam that he lets a loaf of bread burn, Mrs. Morel lashes out at him like a jealous lover, saying, "You only want me to wait on you—the rest is for Miriam." He can't bear to hear his mother talk like that. "Instinctively he realized that he was life to [his mother]. And, after all, she was the chief thing to him, the only supreme thing." So he tells his mother he doesn't love Miriam, not really.

"I talk to her," Paul explains, "but I want to come home to you."

The whole exchange just gets wackier after that, with Mrs. Morel saying:

> "I can't bear it. . . . She'd leave me no room, not a bit of room—"
> And immediately [Paul] hated Miriam bitterly.
> "And I've never—you know, Paul—I've never had a husband—not really—"
> He stroked his mother's hair, and his mouth was on her throat. . . .
> "Well, I don't love her, mother," he murmured. . . . His mother kissed him a
> long, fervent kiss.
> "My boy!" she said, in a voice trembling with passionate love.
> . . . he gently stroked her face.

No way, you think? Impossible that a mother-son relationship would be so overtly sexual? Well, *Sons and Lovers* was supposedly heavily autobiographical.

Back to Lawrence's alter ego: Because Paul does love Miriam—even if not quite as much as he loves his mother—he can't break with her entirely, though he tells his mother he wants to. He and Miriam are on-again, off-again for years. (When people would ask him what the status of the relationship was, I imagine he'd say, "It's complicated.") In the meantime, he manages to get involved with an older woman named Clara Dawes, a friend of Miriam's who works with him at the factory. (He's employed there into adulthood while also trying to make a name for himself as a painter.) A shrewd, unconventional proto-feminist who is separated from her husband, Clara is superficially similar to Mrs. Morel, while being Miriam's opposite: Paul's connection to the girl he's known since childhood is largely intellectual and psychological, while his attraction to Clara is predominantly—at times almost overwhelmingly—physical.

Mrs. Morel is more accepting of Clara than Miriam, perhaps because there's only so far Paul's relationship with a woman who isn't divorced can go. Or else Mrs. Morel understands that Paul is mainly

interested in Clara for sex—and Mrs. Morel might be way too into her son, but even she can draw the line there. In any event, Paul soon grows tired of Clara. Griping about his dissatisfaction to his mother, he says: "I . . . love Clara, and I did Miriam; but to give myself to them in marriage I couldn't. I couldn't belong to them. They seem to want me, and I can't ever give it them. . . . I shall never meet the right woman while you live." (Wow. At least he's in touch with his feelings?)

Mrs. Morel doesn't do much to encourage him to leave the nest; her response is to weakly suggest that he *will* meet someone soon enough, even if he hasn't yet.

As she gets on in years, Mrs. Morel becomes terminally ill. During her months in bed, Paul wonders if her death might be the key to helping him resolve his romantic turbulence; he thinks that if she dies, he might finally be able to move on. So when he and his sister secretly euthanize the older woman by drugging her milk, because it's difficult to see her in so much pain, you have to wonder about Paul's deeper motivations. (Isn't it the *father* who's supposed to get killed in a case like this?) Even after she's physically gone, however, Paul can't shake his mother's hold on his psyche. He briefly returns to Miriam, hoping she might help him out of his misery. Only too willing to take him back, she suggests that the two of them marry so she can "prevent [him from] wasting himself." Despite his agony, he can't accept her offer or glean any real comfort from her. They spend a single night together, but he says good-bye to Miriam the next day, noticing, "his soul could not leave [his mother], wherever she was. . . . he was with her still." The book ends with Paul whimpering, "Mother! Mother!" and thinking, "She was the only thing that held him up. . . ."

Get the feeling he won't be signing up for Match.com any time soon?

If *you* find yourself seeing a bloke who seems suspiciously close to the female head of his family, you may want to mention that you think he'd get a kick out of *Sons and Lovers* while gifting him a copy. If

he can't stop telling how much he relates to Paul and how eerily alike they are, well, perhaps your next recommendation for him should be Freud's *Totem and Taboo*. Maybe you should suggest he take a hike along with it.

But if you're in deep with a guy who always wants to do things his mother's way, instead of *your* way, don't throw the baby out with his maternal bath water. Sure, your approach might be just as good as his mother's; it might even be better. In every relationship, however, compromises are necessary. So take a step back and say to yourself, "Do I really care about what we're debating here, or is this mostly just a power struggle between his mom and me?" If it's the latter, let it go. Be the grown-up if his mother can't.

On the other hand, standing up to the grizzly mama now and then could work in your favor. Your guy might respect you for challenging the woman he's always given in to. When you've got a strong case to make about why your way is actually better, assert yourself. Remain calm. Don't raise your voice. Smile. Thank her profusely for the cream leather living room set she wants to buy you two, just like the ones that are all the rage in her Florida retirement community, but tell her it just doesn't work with the rest of the apartment. Remember that the discussion is about decor and not about which one of you is a better woman. If she can't handle the occasional push-back—*and* her son doesn't protect you from her nonsense—it's worth wondering whether the relationship is worth fighting for. (Do you want to contend with this overweening woman every time you and your dude celebrate a holiday, take a vacation, and consider trying a new dry-cleaner?) But if you and she can have rational discussions, take it as a good indicator that she could come around to seeing you as an equal someday—though she may be hard-pressed to think of her boy as anything but her dependent.

I suppose you could say I "dated" a maternally challenged guy once, Marshall, the only child of divorced wealthy parents. He and

I met while he was visiting some of his high school friends, college pals of mine, at our New England campus. The two of us hit it off big-time, or so I thought through the haze of intoxication. He slept over in my dorm room (though we went only as far as heavy petting, as anyone who has read the chapter on *The Bell Jar* will know). He kissed me in the morning before piling off into the car to the airport. It seemed to me like The Start of Something Big.

A couple months later summer arrived—time for our plan to be together forever to start. I'd landed a West Coast internship, not far from where he'd be for the summer. The idea was that I'd stay in his place for the first week of my sojourn till I could move into my sublet—and we'd spend the subsequent months having a California romance more beautiful than the final scenes of *The Graduate*.

Except . . .

Except I hadn't been out there a full day before he began to irritate me in the extreme. He could not stop talking about *Muh-me* in the most appallingly nasalized way, like he was someone who should be wearing a cravat and a velvet smoking jacket and ordering the butler around. As in, "I told *Muh-me* you were coming in today." And then—as we were getting ready to make dinner that first night—he called her, using some question about the pesto as a pretext, and they chatted away for about fifteen minutes. Though I could be misremembering this, I could almost swear that as they were finally bidding each other adieu, he looked me up and down, saying, "I think you'll like her—although maybe not as much as you liked Susie."

I slept on the couch and arranged to move into my sublet the next day—and that was the end of that mama's boy.

LOVE'S
LABORS
FOUND

Making It Work

TO THE DOGHOUSE

How to Deal with Unfeeling Men

ACCORDING TO JACK

I love the concept of emotional intelligence: The fact that psychologists and philosophers finally figured out that the ability to feel and comprehend emotions in ourselves and others isn't just a nice social trait but an actual cognitive skill—and a vital component to a human being's all-around "smarts."

How many people do we know who have some hypertrophied intellectual ability but no understanding of interpersonal relations, how humans tick, how to treat other people well, etc. etc.? And based on the reports of my female friends out there in the dating trenches, sometimes it seems as if this all right-brain, no left-brain group should just be called "men."

Take the excellent case study we find in Virginia Woolf's *To the Lighthouse*, where a woman of extreme emotional intelligence struggles to understand and cope with her philosopher husband, who's a brilliant logical and abstract thinker but an utter clunker in the touchy-feely sciences. Woolf is one of the most sensitive and profound researchers into human psychology that literature (and perhaps the world) has known, and it's fascinating to see how her protagonist Mrs. Ramsay negotiates the fact that Mr. Ramsay can be simultaneously so

seemingly intelligent and yet such a dunce. Somehow I think pretty much all you women out there (and maybe many of you men), will find or will have already found yourself in a similar position, wondering how to get through to someone who seems to see our intricate Technicolor emotional world in the most lifeless of black and white.

The novel takes its title from the question of whether the Ramsay family is going to take a trip from their summer home in the Hebrides to the nearby lighthouse, with the lighthouse itself eventually becoming a symbol of a kind of self-sufficiency that few if any of the characters possess. The Ramsay family has eight children, and the six-year-old son, James, is especially keen on going. The book begins with Mrs. Ramsay saying, "Yes, of course, if [the weather] is fine tomorrow"—words that, to her son, "conveyed an extraordinary joy, as if it were settled, the expedition were bound to take place, and the wonder to which he had looked forward, for years and years it seemed was . . . within touch."

Turn the page, however, and the husband says flatly, "But it won't be fine."

And, in a paragraph that echoes what we will hear Anna Karenina say about her husband, Mrs. Ramsay thinks: "What he said was true. It was always true. He was incapable of untruth; never tampered with a fact; never altered a disagreeable word to suit the pleasure or convenience of any mortal being, least of all his own children, who, sprung from his loins, should be aware from childhood that life is difficult."

In other words, he was utterly lacking in emotional intelligence and the sympathy to realize that humans should take precedence over always being perfectly accurate. In still other words, he's one of those know-it-all wanker types who correct everything everyone says, regardless of the context. Ever met one of those?

Mrs. Ramsay, meanwhile, is the exact opposite and still tries to save the day for her son by saying, "But it may be fine—I expect it to be fine."

She's attempting to placate the boy who already feels like he wants to kill his father. A good mother, she can't help but be considerate, not only of her son, but of all people. Like many women seem to, Mrs. Ramsay "had the whole of the other sex under her protection." Men, she thinks, "negotiated treaties, ruled India, controlled finance," but she took care of them.

But can I say, being one of the gender in question, isn't it about time we learn to take care of ourselves—and, even more, take care of the Mrs. Ramsays a little?

Sadly, the men in *To the Lighthouse* have no such sympathy. The other guy present, Charles Tansey, also an academic, feels the need to contradict her as well: "There will be no landing at the lighthouse tomorrow." Dudes! Enough!

The scene is nicely layered: Not only is Woolf demonstrating how insensitive the men are to the little boy's feelings and needs, but she's also skewering them for how confidently they assert their supposed knowledge, despite the fact that they're talking about the *next day's weather*! I myself have noticed, many times in my life, how saying something forcefully with trumped-up conviction will get many people to assume that they're wrong and I must be right; I've also noticed many times that women would hear me do that, while knowing for an absolute fact that I was wrong, but still not say anything. Moral of the story: If you women want us to stop b.s.-ing so much, start calling us out on it more!

Mrs. Ramsay isn't ready to do that yet, so instead she reiterates that she'd like to get the stockings she's knitting to the lighthouse keeper's boy tomorrow. In return her husband "snapped out irascibly" that "there wasn't the slightest possible chance that they could go to the lighthouse tomorrow." "How did he know?" she asks, pointing out that "the wind often changed."

It's a fabulous setup because, when you think about it, they're really both right: There's very little chance of them going, but there is

still some possibility. And so it goes with truth, much of the time, not an either-or as some scientists would have it, but a both-and, depending on perspective, emphasis, need, and many other all too human factors. How many times have we thought back on arguments we've had in relationships and realized that, right as we might have been in our point, the other person was right in theirs, too?

As a young man, I, like Mr. Ramsay, occupied myself with philosophy and thought there were clear rights and wrongs to every situation and that I—not luckily, only deservedly—was in sole possession of the answers. The sad part, by contrast, is that Mrs. Ramsay, as a mother of eight and wife to one, is probably wiser than I'll ever be, but her behavior is almost the opposite, frequently doubting not only her opinions, but even her self-worth. She "often felt she was nothing but a sponge sopped up of human emotions . . . She was not good enough to tie [her husband's] shoestrings, she thought."

But this is precisely what women *shouldn't* think! As I suggested earlier, the more you capitulate, outwardly or sotto voce, the more we men will continue to think that our behavior is not only acceptable but right. It's our trick to keep plowing forward and assume that you will eventually doubt yourselves and give in to us—and, sadly, it often works.

I know why it happens; I know that men tend to be conditioned to think we're always right and women tend to be conditioned the other way. I know that when women do become assertive, they often scare guys away. But good riddance, I say! If a guy puts his tail between his legs and scampers off because you were willing to tell him when he was wrong or limited in his thinking, then you should slam the door after him. (And, yes, I realize this would reduce the dating pool even more, but there are some things you really shouldn't have to compromise.)

Ultimately I think Woolf gets it right; she speaks of the "fatal sterility of the male . . . like a beak of brass, barren and bare," and

by this I think she means men's thinking when devoid of emotional intelligence. She contemplates her husband and wants "his senses restored to him, his barrenness made fertile" instead of him simply having that "beak of brass, the arid scimitar of the male, which smote mercilessly." Woolf repeats this platypus of a mixed metaphor one more time ("the beak of brass, the arid scimitar of his father, the egotistical man, plunged and smote"—uh, *calling Dr. Freud. Dr. Freud, are you with us?*)—to underscore Mrs. Ramsay's frustration one more time. Why can't her husband understand?

Mrs. Ramsay knows that there are more things in heaven and earth than are dreamt of in Horatio's (or Mr. Ramsay's) philosophy; he just doesn't see it because he doesn't have a vestige of the emotional intelligence she has.

But what traps her, ultimately, is the sense that "she did not like, even for a second, to feel finer than her husband." I'm sorry, though—when the slipper fits, and often it will, then I think it's a woman's duty to stand up for herself, for what she believes in, and to put the guy in his place. And if that means she loses respect for him, then maybe he never deserved that respect in the first place.

Maura says:

I couldn't agree with Jack more: If you think a guy is talking poppycock, let him know. It's one thing if the two of you have differing political opinions on matters that don't affect your day-to-day life (like, oh, I don't know, gun control) and you've agreed *not* to discuss them because you know you'll never see eye to eye. But *never* automatically cede ground just because he's louder and more forceful. You have a right to your ideas. (And if you discover you can't defend your position too well, admit that—and do your research

for the next time. A lot of blowhards don't know much more about any given issue than what they've read in some newspaper or gleaned from a Google search.) Do not let a guy steamroll over you, because if he does it once, he'll do it again and again—till you're leveled completely.

Conversely, by defending your point of view in any given matter, you'll gain some personal strength. And though there are some guys who are so insecure and provincial that they can't deal with a woman who speaks her mind—and Jack is right when he says you're better off without those losers—a *lot* of men are quite appreciative, even delighted, when you challenge a point they've made or inform them that they're being ridiculous in some way. Peruse the online dating sites, in fact, and you'll find that a surprising number of men actually state in their profiles that they want a girl who's capable of calling them out from time to time.

Why would that be appealing? I think it has to do with the male love of competition. Men see women who push back a little as more of a "challenge." (And unlike playing hard to get, giving someone a little feedback or sass is a healthy way of being challenging; when you do that, you're not playing manipulative games, but learning to have a more truthful give-and-take.) Then again, maybe the explanation is simpler: It can be reassuring to find someone who isn't afraid of speaking the truth, because you'll always know where you stand with her.

RABBIT, RUN SCREAMING

The Problem of Boredom in Marriage

ACCORDING TO JACK

Rabbit Angstrom is John Updike's great fictional character, the protagonist of four interconnected novels and a novella (*Rabbit, Run; Rabbit Redux; Rabbit Is Rich; Rabbit at Rest;* and *Rabbit Remembered*) and his primary vehicle for depiction of everyday life in the American 'burbs. The first novel, *Rabbit, Run*, is a kind of early 1960s *Desperate Househus-band*, as the barely employed Rabbit, sent by his pregnant wife to go pick up their two-year-old boy from his parents, goes to get the car, turns the key, has a moment of realization, and heads out of town, intending not to return.

It's a flight from discord, from ennui, from responsibility, and from reality. Rabbit (whose real name is Harry) once lived the dream: He's a former high school basketball star, the golden boy of his town, but now he's been reduced to a standard humdrum existence. And yet he's still built to run—in pretty much every way—and when he's stressed or overwhelmed, he takes off, either literally or figuratively, and, sadly, at this point in his development, the circumstances of his life frequently get the best of him.

Foremost of his problems is his domestic situation, sent into crisis by his sudden realization that he's past the breaking point with

his wife. When the novel begins, he's coming home from his job peddling electric vegetable peelers, stops to play pickup ball with a bunch of teenagers (despite being in a business suit), trounces them, then comes down from that high and the feeling of a "fresh chance in the air" only to open his front door and find Janice, his wife, drunk as usual, "sitting in an armchair with an Old-fashioned, watching television." Within a page, he thinks about as damning a flash impression as you can possibly have about your spouse: "Just yesterday, it seems to him, she stopped being pretty"—eeks!

But truthfully, their problems are much more than skin deep. When he walks in on Janice, she's watching the Mouseketeers, though their son isn't there, and later she turns off the set when the news comes on. Rabbit finally concludes to himself something he'll repeat a number of times: "She is dumb."

And then there's alcohol—because Janice is well on her way to Kitty Dukakis-dom—and the sex now, apparently, is "always an effort." He's at wit's end and worse still, he begins to suspect that it's not likely to get any better: "He keeps getting the feeling . . . of her only going one way, toward deeper wrinkles and thinner hair." It's bad, and it's only going to deteriorate.

Sensing how upset he is with her, Janice prophetically says, "Don't run from me, Harry. I love you." But when she sends him out for cigarettes and to pick up their son, Harry's condition is summed up by Updike this way: "He is in a trap. It seems certain. He goes out."

The final straw comes when he sees his son through a window of his parents' house, sees how his mother is trying to get the little boy to eat, and realizes, "This home is happier than his." From that point, he wants to go. He gets in the car and heads for the highway, leaving behind his boy and his pregnant, jobless wife.

Now, we can probably all agree that running out on your spouse and family is unconscionable in virtually every instance. But who among us hasn't had this kind of fantasy of flight, whether it's from a

family, a relationship, or even just a boss you want to tell to high-step it to Hades? And what's nice about *Rabbit, Run* is how clearly we can see the buildup to Rabbit's eventual snap, how the ever-present threat of boredom in a marriage is laid bare, and then we can try to learn from it, to reduce the risk of it happening to us.

It's clear that long relationships receive double attention on time's blackboard: Wrinkles are scribbled on us with one hand just as the dynamism and spark of early infatuation is erased with the other. We age, but so, too, do the novelty, exhilaration, and often the effort that mark the beginnings of romance. And then perhaps you wake up one day like Rabbit, agonizingly conscious that you don't find your partner attractive, or that the sex doesn't come easily, or that one or both of you is numbing it all with alcohol, or that you feel bound and trapped and hopeless. In marriage, complacency is clearly a killer, the steady taking for granted of all the things for which you should be grateful, for which you should give back, and from which you could take strength. Habit numbs us, so we have to try to remind ourselves again and again to keep trying, to stay committed, and to put in effort.

For me, the difficulty arises in maintaining the pace I set early in relationships. Right out of the gate, I'm on a sprint for affection, to give as much love as possible and be as good a boyfriend as I can in hopes that I'll be liked, even loved, back. After a year or two, it's hard for me to stay as assiduous; the will wanes a bit, but unfortunately I've set patterns and expectations that, if I don't keep them up, will cause pain for the other person. In a recent relationship, my girlfriend of two years realized she had never filled her own water glass at my apartment much less been allowed to do a dish, throw something away, or make a cup of tea. Some part of me had tried to treat her like a princess to the point where she'd become habituated to doing nothing at all. Bad move on my part—great for seduction, maybe, but horrible if you want to keep a relationship strong for the long haul.

I have a friend who takes a very different approach: He tries to do nothing in the early stages of romance that he wouldn't want to do *for forty straight years!* No flowers for you, honey; I don't want to be stuck doing that every week for the rest of my life! Fancy dinners, doing the dishes, surprise trips on Valentine's? Not from me! That's more or less what his behavior says, but sure enough, he's happily married while I'm still single. (And, yes, I'm *quite* bitter about it!)

So I'll admit that his tortoise approach probably works better ultimately than my hare's, but who doesn't want to get swept away in early infatuation? And who doesn't also keep up hope that the people we are when we first love someone—those incarnations that often feel like the best versions of ourselves we could be—might just be able to be maintained forever?

But for them to have any chance of enduring—and for the relationship to stay vital and fulfilling for a protracted period—I think we have to realize that many of the things that buoy new love will diminish over time and that it's our job to replace them with other things that will compensate. Companionship, trust, evolved sex, real support, deep understanding, and care—these are things that need years of nurturing. If you work for them, I think they can counterbalance the fact that your partner isn't quite as firm and smooth as she once was or your patience for him isn't as strong as at the beginning, and perhaps you sleep together less frequently (but hopefully with greater understanding and intimacy). Let having sex fully transform into making love. Let familiarity breed contact, not contempt.

For Rabbit, that was far from the case, and he ultimately drives as far as West Virginia before he becomes haunted by what an old farmer-type had said to him while pumping his gas: "The only way to get somewhere is to figure out where you're going before you go there."

Of course that's not true, but when Rabbit misreads his map, makes a few wrong turns, and loses track of where he is, the absurdity

of his situation—or perhaps the reality—begins to sink in, and he tears up the map and heads back toward home (though not yet to his wife).

I don't want to spoil how it unfolds, but trust me when I say that Rabbit does in fact keep running—from one reality he's fed up with or doesn't understand to another he thinks will be better, then to another, then back and back once more. Time and again, though, he feels "the difficulty of pleasing someone" beginning to "hem him in." He struggles to address his relationships head-on, to put the work into them that they really do require—both working through difficulties and working to keep yourself investing and trying.

Instead he makes the mistake of thinking that it's over, that with marriage and children come the death of the self. In his nostalgic, glory-days worldview, he sums it up like this: "He feels the truth the thing that has left his life has left irrevocably . . . The fullness ends when we give Nature her ransom, when we make children for her. Then she is through with us, and we become, first inside, and then outside, junk."

What could be the joy of love and family instead feels like the final abandonment of self. How sad—and how avoidable.

Chapter 28

MADAME HO-VARY

Is Cheating Ever Okay?

ACCORDING TO JACK

What would it take for it to be okay to run around on your spouse? Can infidelity ever be justified?

Part of me wants to say no because, by nature, I'm a one-woman man. (Yes, I've done my fair share of dallying, but whenever I've been in something serious and monogamous, I didn't have any problems staying true. That said, I've also never been married. . . .)

Another part of me also wants to say no because I tend to think that cheating—especially men's cheating—often has more to do with weaknesses in the cheater than weaknesses in the person cheated on or even in the relationship.

That said, I'm not a hard-liner in all circumstances. I've known a number of women who have cheated on their husbands, and since I tend to think that men are responsible for mussing up most of the things in this world (though I know that's not entirely the case), I have a default sympathy for women who stray in their marriages. I assume that their beaus must be brutes, that they are held back by them and by society and by all the other problems that plague women (and that guys like me tend to feel guilty about), and that they must be in the right.

Take the example of one woman I know. For more than four years she hadn't gotten any loving from her husband, but apart from that, their relationship was good. She didn't have money or a career of her own, so leaving him would be very tricky economically. Plus they had a number of kids, and she didn't want to demolish a pretty happy family.

What was she supposed to do? If you're suffering through a loveless, sexless marriage but have legitimate reasons for not getting out of it, what are your options? Isn't everyone entitled to a little affection?

It's hard not to think that if one's partner becomes severely neglectful physically or emotionally, infidelity might be just what he or she deserves. Clearly, cheating on someone is horrible in most cases, but perhaps there really are situations where the person who strays is justified.

But how do you separate affairs that can perhaps be condoned—at least from some perspectives—from those that are merely spiritual failing and bad decision making? One way is to examine the stories of the two most famous unfaithful ladies in Western literature, the title characters from Flaubert's *Madame Bovary* (1856) and Tolstoy's *Anna Karenina* (1877).

In some ways the novels are quite similar, but if you read them attentively, you might come away, as I did, finding sympathy for one of the women but thinking the other one rather repulsive.

In the Russian heroine's case, she was married to a flat, soul-deadening goody-goody. I'll go further into it in the Manna Karenina chapter, but suffice it to say that her home life would have been great for a cactus but not for something that needed any amount of love and attention.

Meanwhile, Emma Bovary's home life wasn't ideal, but at least it was a little better. Her husband, Charles, a family doctor, is your basic enthusiastic, loving husband, though admittedly he's "anything but quick-witted." That said, Emma was clearly attracted to him before

their marriage; she flirted with him when he made calls to her house, as we know by the way she suggestively licked droplets out of the bottom of her aperitif glass.

After the marriage, however, and despite all his attentions, she simply started to get bored. Flaubert chalks it up to Emma having read too many romantic novels, such that she "tried to find out what one meant exactly in life by the words bliss, passion, ecstasy, that seemed to her so beautiful in books."

Now, I'm never one to begrudge someone else's disappointment with life (Weltschmerz runs deep in my blood, too), but Emma does nothing whatsoever to try to improve her relations with Charles. Instead, she simply gets more and more impatient until she finally asks herself, "Why, for Heaven's sake, did I marry" and "no longer concealed her contempt for anything or anybody, and . . . longed for lives of adventure, for masked balls, for shameless pleasures."

In my last book, I said that Flaubert's use of the word "shameless" in that quote is a tip-off that Emma isn't quite the suffering heroine she's normally thought of as being. I'm quite convinced that Flaubert meant to be critical of her adultery, and I think the text bears it out. Look at how she behaves when she meets Leon, a stranger in an inn who will eventually become her lover: The Bovarys are sharing a public table with him, when Leon comments that the lady must be tired from traveling, and the very first words out of our heroine's mouth are already flirtatious! "'That is true,' replied Emma, 'but moving about always amuses me. I like change.'" Leon's response, of course, is in a similar vein: "'It is so tedious,' sighed the clerk, 'to always be riveted to the same places.'" But she hasn't even been married a year! How is that riveted?

No, Emma Bovary is not a victim, she's simply flighty. Soon after she gives birth to her daughter, Berthe, she grows tired of motherhood; it, too, does not live up to her imagination.

So when she finally meets Rodolphe, a rake who immediately

decides to seduce her but then wonders "how to get rid of her afterwards," she is easily taken in by his criticisms of their provincial town and "the lives it stifles." Emma, for her part, adds that when one is in the country, as she is, "nothing is worth while." Nothing? Really? Nothing at all? See what I mean about her being spoiled and capricious and unwilling to make an effort?

Rodolphe gets his way, of course, and, while they continue seeing each other on the sly for quite some time, eventually he jilts her right before she is to leave her husband and run away with him. (For the record, this is how seemingly extremely romantic infidelities tend to end in real life, too, if they don't simply peter out.)

From there, it's equally predictable: Emma gets ill; almost dies; finds religion briefly; considers killing herself; gets back together with Leon; soon becomes bored with him, too; gets her husband, Charles, deep in debt by buying clothes; and eventually, when the creditors call, she does in fact commit suicide, leaving her husband in ruin.

Are we to feel sympathy?

At her most innocent, when she says things like, "If only you knew all I dreamed," it's hard not to be on her side, hard not to imagine her as generations of readers seem to: a striving, ambitious dreamer who broke out of society's constraints and was ultimately punished for it. But you know what? That's not what's going on here.

Here's the quote I always reference when I want to rest my case that Flaubert didn't like his heroine (despite famously saying, "Madame Bovary . . . *c'est moi!*"). It takes place right after Emma has killed herself: (and note the scorn and derision, the absolute indictment of her lasciviousness and concupiscence). "The priest . . . began to give extreme unction. First, upon the eyes, that had so coveted all worldly goods; then upon the nostrils, that had been so greedy of the warm breeze and the scents of love; then upon the mouth, that had spoken lies, moaned in pride and cried out in lust; then upon the hands that had taken delight in the texture of sensuality; and finally upon the

soles of the feet, so swift when she had hastened to satisfy her desires, and that would now walk no more."

Feel any pity now? Whereas Anna Karenina's husband was a sanctimonious jerk who actively made Anna's life hell, Charles Bovary was just lame. And instead of trying to find anything interesting in him or developing their relationship, Emma simply grabbed after anything she saw (the impulse which led her to marry him in the first place). Anna Karenina wasn't just dying at home; she was being killed. Her affair *was* necessary—and forgivable. Emma Bovary's was the opposite.

And so, too, then, in real life. Clearly there are bad marriages, and the first priority of a victim of a bad spouse is to attempt to put an end to it. That might not always be possible, but clearly (as we'll see discussing Anna Karenina), one shouldn't have to live a joyless life, no matter how bad a partnership you entered into.

That said, most people who cheat are more like Emma Bovary: selfish, weak, and unwilling either to fix a bad situation or to put an end to it.

So look to your relationship and see what you're really up to. Unloved, untended to, but unable to get a divorce? Perhaps then infidelity is your only choice. But if you can either fix or end your relationship instead, it's hard to see how cheating would be the better option.

When infidelity is the easy way out instead of the *only* way out, it probably can't be justified.

MANNA KARENINA

What If a Lover Just Drops from the Sky?

ACCORDING TO JACK

Reader, there will be temptations. Sadly—or perhaps not so sadly—there will always eventually be the mechanic with the heavy wrench, the grocer with the impressive pomegranates, or even just your best friend's spouse—gasp!—who dials up your daydreams, making you consider the road untaken and giving you a little jolt that is often far from comfortable or welcome.

Our species evolved from quadrupeds, and you see how they act.

But, as I wrote in the *Oscar Wao* chapter, the good news for us higher organisms is that we don't have to act on our lower impulses. We have the power of reflection and discernment, the ability to weigh probable outcomes and effects, to look deeper into the problem and see if our sudden lust is just that—lust—or the sign of something else. And then we can put it back in our metaphorical pants and move on.

Because you know what? Cheating tends to stink. Affairs usually disappoint. The grass doesn't stay greener on the other side.

Why would it? Take, for instance, the famous affair launched into by our dear friend Anna Karenina. We've talked about her in the preceding chapter, concluding that her marriage might have actually been

awful enough to justify running around (where Emma Bovary's or Yunior de Las Casas's weren't). But just so you can see why, here's how she sums up her husband and her awful domestic state:

> *The mean, disgusting man! And no one understands it except me. No one will ever understand it. And I can't explain it. They say, "Oh, he's such a religious, moral, honest, intelligent man!" But they don't see what I've seen. They don't know how for eight years he has crushed my life, crushed every-thing that was alive in me, that he has never once thought that I was a live woman who was in need of love. They do not know how at every step he has slighted me and remained self-satisfied. Haven't I tried, tried with all my might, to find some kind of justification for my life? Haven't I tried to love him, to love my son when I could no longer love my husband? But the time came when I realized that I couldn't deceive myself any longer, that I was alive, that I couldn't be blamed that God had made me so, that I have to love and live.*

To love and live—those seem like pretty fair things to ask for from this human existence, right? For me at least, it's not hard to feel like Anna is justified in seeking out the love she isn't getting at home.

But—and here's where the other shoe drops—even if she's justi-fied in seeking such things, you miss part of the syllogism if you think that having an affair is going to provide that for her. Sure, we're all entitled to life and love, but is cheating really the way to get those things? I don't want to spoil the book for those of you who haven't read it, but let's just say that her little fling with Vronsky doesn't turn out exactly as Anna hoped.

Still, without giving away too much, let's follow her story a little so that if, in your life, a lover seems to fall from the heavens like an Armani suit full of manna, you will ask yourself a few questions be-fore you decide to partake. Yes, the doorbell will ring, but if it's only the postman, as they say, he'll ring again.

What amazes me is that people who cheat don't seem to ask themselves what kind of person wants to have an affair with someone who is married. Aren't they likely to be a certain type?

In Anna's case, the man in question is the young rake Vronsky, who, at the time he meets Anna is in the midst of misleading another major female character in the novel, Kitty. He's on the verge of jilting her and ruining her reputation, but in his mind he's just doing what seems natural. As Tolstoy puts it: "He did not realize that his behavior toward Kitty had a name of its own, that it was the seduction of a girl without the intention of marrying her, and that this kind of seduction is the sort of reprehensible thing common among brilliant young men like himself. He imagined that he was the first to discover the pleasure, and he enjoyed his discovery to the full."

Unfortunately, I know from experience that this is the kind of guy (or even woman) you're likely to get when you run around—someone who enjoys the chase but isn't that interested in keeping what he has caught. The times in my life when I've been with married women—and I can't say I'm proud of them—were in situations where I needed to keep my heart guarded and selfishly didn't want the responsibility of something real. Even if it's not at a conscious level, the person getting involved with someone married probably wants to keep one foot out the door, and that's not the kind of lover you want to risk everything for.

And even if you did end up risking it, what are you hoping to get? Why do we assume that acting on the fantasy actually lives up to the fantasy itself?

This is the part that I believe people don't think about enough. Sure, in your mind, the affair is going to be excellent: The sex will be passionate and fulfilling, you'll adore each other, you'll renew your sense of adventure, and of course you'll never get caught or hurt anyone's feelings. But how can you be so certain? Even the sex isn't likely

to be that special—how often is it with someone new? And think how much you've invested in it being *great*—is it likely to live up to that?

In Anna and Vronsky's case, we don't get to know exactly how it went, but the aftermath sure wasn't pretty.

> *"Oh God, forgive me!" she said, sobbing . . . Looking at him, she felt her degradation physically and she could not utter another word. He felt what a murderer must feel when he looks at the body he has deprived of life . . . There was something dreadful and loathsome in the recollection of what had been paid for by this terrible price of shame . . . [as] the murderer throws himself on the body with a feeling of bitter resentment and as though with passion, and drags it off and cuts it to pieces; so he, too, covered her face and shoulders with kisses.*

Uh, that's not good.

But say you're having illicit thoughts about someone other than your partner. What are you supposed to do?

I know that the New Testament says that to sin in thought is the same as sinning in life, but all modern psychologists postulate the opposite. According to them, it's entirely natural to fantasize about a lot of stuff you might like to do in reality (but probably won't) and even about stuff that you would *never* do for real.

No one knows why, but our brains are capable of some pretty dark thoughts, yet it is the privilege of having free will that allows us to keep those where they belong: as fantasy.

An interesting—and often overlooked element in this as well—is how acting out your imagination can actually ruin the thing you've been dreaming about. Ever have a threesome? A lot of us have wanted to and thought how incredibly great it would be, but most of the time, *les ménages* are awkward and disappointing and don't come close to living up to their billing. And what happens after? Your

idealization of them becomes tainted, so they're less fun to fantasize about. Reality can kill fantasy, and that's never a good thing.

For Anna, she needed to recognize that the jolt she felt when she would see Vronsky wouldn't necessarily translate into happiness with him in her arms. In the early stages of the courtship, Tolstoy says that "there was nothing unpleasant or gloomy about . . . the visions which filled her imagination; on the contrary, there was something joyful, glowing, and exhilarating in it."

As you can guess, she could have kept that exhilarated feeling longer by not acting on it. Because think about it: What happens when the novelty wears off?

No long relationship begins without a certain amount of dynamism and excitement. And, yes, that energy often fades over time, and it's the work of both parties in a marriage to try to keep it alive. In Anna's, it was long gone, and Vronsky represented to her the possibility of finding true love, a love, she tells him, that "meant too much" to her, "much more than [he] could understand."

But say you do leave your spouse for your new lover, as Anna ultimately does. Won't time take its toll on this new relationship? Won't you notice eventually how in the early days his idiosyncrasies were charming, but now they've grown wearisome? Yes, there are affairs that grow into great loves, but much more often the same lassitude and disillusion that plagued the marriage will come to plague its replacement. Despite what all the love songs say, the key to success is often less about whom you are with and more about *how* you're with them.

That means that the most important question might very well be whether anything can be done to improve things at home.

In Anna's case, probably not, but of course that doesn't go for everyone. The person feeling the impulse to be unfaithful does well to look to him or herself first and see if the problems begin there. Often infidelity happens for reasons that have nothing to do with the relationship, yet it threatens to hurt the other person irrevocably.

As Anna and Vronsky's relationship makes clear—and as reality bears out again and again—infidelity is ultimately a kind of gamble, only the stakes are somewhat perverse: What you risk losing is so much greater than what you are likely to win, it's hard to see how anyone would do it. If only we could all see the odds before we imperiled everything, life would be full of many fewer Anna Kareninas and Emma Bovarys.

As it stands, people go out and roll those same dice again and again. What a pity.

BLEAK HOUSE? NOT THIS ONE

Dickens's Recipe for the Perfect Marriage

ACCORDING TO JACK

I'll admit it; I'm a complete softie. Yes, that would be me, blubbering through *Wall-E* because it tears me up when anyone—even a fictitious cartoon trash-compactor—feels alone and unloved. Yes, that's me having to keep from ever walking by the animal shelter in my neighborhood, knowing that if I saw any abandoned dog in the window, I'd immediately take him home. Even thrown-away plants that I see on the street tend to make it back to my apartment—it's a kind of sanctuary for the cast off—and though they don't all get nursed back to health, many do.

The reason for all this, obviously, is I just want everything to be cared for. I firmly believe that nothing on this planet was meant to be alone—nope, not even you, Ted Kaczynski!—and so it breaks my heart to see anyone missing out on the experience of sharing with another.

Thus one of my all-time favorite things to see is an old couple walking hand in hand down the sidewalk. He has his rakish fedora; she's wrapped in her babushka; they are arm in arm and clearly have been for decades. And when he reaches over to kiss the lips of his wife (they're now the same height), you can tell there's still a spark,

he's still grateful, and they're clearly both warm and loving and happy. Is there anything better than that?

Of course I know from experience that married old people tend to grouse about each other almost continuously, but I also know that they grow inseparable, that their lives and even identities are formed entirely around the companionship, and that it's common that when one dies, the other, even if he or she is in good health, will die soon after.

I want to be in that kind of couple; I want to be able to stay with one person until I'm old enough to finally wear all the bow ties I bought in high school (NOT a good way to promote getting a future bride, as it turned out). I want to lean over and look at my wife and have my eyes full of sparkle, loving her and knowing I'll always love her.

That's why my favorite couple in all of literature is the Bagnets from what is often called Charles Dickens's best novel: *Bleak House.*

The Bagnets are minor characters in the great London theater that is *Bleak House,* but no writer has ever done bit players quite like Dickens, and they really are an enormous treat. Here's how he introduces us to the missus:

> *Mrs. Bagnet is not at all an ill-looking woman. Rather large-boned, a little coarse in the grain, and freckled by the sun and wind which have tanned her hair upon the forehead; but healthy, wholesome, and bright-eyed. A strong, busy, active, honest-faced woman . . . clean, hardy, and so economically dressed (though substantially), that the only article of ornament of which she stands possessed appears to be her wedding ring; around which her finger has grown to be so large since it was put on, that it will never come off again until it shall mingle with Mrs. Bagnet's dust.*

I love that description, and not only because she reminds me of my Romanian great-grandmother, who was married to her husband

for more than sixty years. I love the metaphor of the ring—obvious though it is—and I further love Mrs. Bagnet because she's so no-nonsense and appreciative of all the things life provides, as this passage bears out: "Boiled beef and greens constitute the day's variety on the former repast of boiled pork and greens; and Mrs. Bagnet serves out the meal in the same way, and seasons it with the best of temper: being that rare sort of old girl that she receives Good to her arms without a hint that it might be Better; and catches light from any little spot of darkness near her."

Mrs. Bagnet adds to God's bounty just by embracing it all. Mr. Bagnet, meanwhile, is no different himself, a no-frills life-lover and more in love with—and respecting of—his wife than any character I've ever read. Here's Dickens's description of Bagnet and his booming voice (the secret to their relationship we'll see in a second): "Mr. Bagnet is an ex-artilleryman, tall and upright, with shaggy eyebrows and whiskers like the fibres of a cocoanut, not a hair upon his head, and a torrid complexion. His voice, short, deep, and resonant, is not at all unlike the tones of the instrument to which he is devoted. Indeed there may be generally observed in him an unbending, unyielding, brass-bound air, as if he were himself the bassoon of the human orchestra."

In other words, they're pretty much the coarsest salt of the earth, adding depth and flavor to everything they come in contact with. But apart from their bonhomie and sanguine approach to life as it is, what we can really learn from them is how to stay in love. Here are their three great tricks:

I. Complete appreciation

Mr. Bagnet *adores* his wife. When his friend George remarks that she looks "as fresh as a rose, and as sound as an apple," Bagnet says the "old girl" (as he calls her—not a good idea unless you've been together a few decades):

> "... is a thoroughly fine woman. Consequently, she is like a thoroughly fine day. Gets finer as she gets on. I never saw the old girl's equal."

> ... "She's worth her weight in gold," returns the trooper.

> "In gold?" says Mr. Bagnet. "I'll tell you what ... the old girl's metal is far more precious—than the preciousest metal ... Think as high of the old girl—as the rock of Gibraltar—and still you'll be thinking low. She's Colour-Serjeant of the Nonpareil battalion."

Yes, I'm a complete sucker for the sentimental, but isn't that one of the sweetest descriptions of a partner you've ever read? Once you've found the person you start to feel that way about—and, maybe even more important, who feels that way about you—you know you're on to something.

2. Trusting the other one's opinion

That last tip was pretty straightforward, but Dickens gives us a more subtle nicety to the Bagnets' relationship in the clever artifice the mister uses to be able to have the missus make important decisions for both of them—without him losing face, as might have been the case in nineteenth-century England (or even today).

See how this scene plays out, as George, the trooper, knows the routine and plays it perfectly:

> Mr. Bagnet requests the trooper to state his case.
> This, Mr. George does with great discretion; appearing to address himself to Mr. Bagnet, but having an eye solely on the old girl all the time, as Bagnet has himself. She, equally discreet, busies herself with her needlework. The case fully stated, Mr. Bagnet resorts to his standard artifice ...
> "That's the whole of it, is it, George?" says he.

"That's the whole of it."

"You'll act according to my opinion?"

"I shall be guided," replies George, *"entirely by it."*

"Old girl," says Mr. Bagnet, *"give him my opinion. You know it. Tell him what it is."*

In a nutshell, when called to speak on business, emotions, or anything of real consequence, Mr. Bagnet says that his wife articulates his opinions better than he does and has her pronounce, knowing full well that she's the wiser one and he's going to want to go with whatever she says.

It warms my heart—and teaches my intellect—to see a man trusting his wife that much. I'm not saying you have to let her make all the decisions (obviously), but if you find yourself with someone who you believe in implicitly—and who believes in you implicitly right back—then you have the basis for an amazing and probably lifelong relationship.

3. Trying to make things nice

The last of the Bagnet tricks is perhaps the most pragmatic of all: simply going out of your way to make things as pleasant as you can for the other person. Dickens, in his infinite wisdom and humor, sets up this element of the Bagnets' relationship but does so in reverse: Yes, Mr. Bagnet goes *way* out of his way each year on his wife's birthday, going so far as to shop for the special chickens for dinner and even cooking them himself. But, not knowing what he's doing, he is of course fleeced by the butcher into buying "the oldest inhabitants of any coop in Europe" and returns

with these triumphs of toughness tied up in a clean blue and white cotton handkerchief (essential to the arrangements) [and] in a casual manner

invites Mrs. Bagnet to declare at breakfast what she would like for dinner. Mrs. Bagnet, by a coincidence never known to fail, replying Fowls, Mr. Bagnet instantly produces his bundle from a place of concealment, amidst general amazement and rejoicing. He further requires that the old girl shall do nothing all day long, but sit in her very best gown, and be served by himself and the young people. As he is not illustrious for his cookery, this may be supposed to be a matter of state rather than enjoyment on the old girl's part; but she keeps her state with all imaginable cheerfulness.

The last line gives us the wink to what's really going on: Mrs. Bagnet, knowing that her husband is going to make an absolute disaster of dinner, sits by cheerfully, making sure things are pleasant for him and seeing the intention behind the bumbling. Though she is "itching to prevent what she sees going wrong," she stays quiet and lets the birds burn.

I've always thought that the key to a relationship lasting is being able to trust that the other person loves us, and thus when he torches the chickens, shows up late, forgets an anniversary, or flies off the handle, we are capable of remembering that he's not doing it to hurt us and that something else must be at play. He's weak, he's struggling, he's unhappy, but he loves us and is probably still trying in whatever way he can. And if we help him, hold him, and, most important, don't take it personally, then we can get through the moment with all parties seeing that the love and commitment can handle a few road bumps. We might even conclude that we really are right for each other.

And maybe then, growing old, we'll turn to our beloved on her birthday and say to the assembled guests what Mrs. Bagnet's husband says of her (year after year): "Take a day's march and you won't find such another. Here's towards her!"

Long live the Bagnets' love—and let's do our best to love like them.

Chapter 31

COWARD'S END

What Happens If You Sacrifice Your Politics for Love?

ACCORDING TO MAURA

For most of my life, I was sure that I'd never be able to date someone whose political outlook differed significantly from mine. Whenever I'd encounter a dude like that, no matter how appealing he might otherwise have been, I didn't have the sense of comfort and communion that I think we're all looking for in a partner. My political views are based on certain fundamental beliefs that I'm strongly convinced are right—and it's hard not to think a guy with vastly different ideas is, well, *wrong*. Just as much as I wouldn't want heavy metal blasting in any home of mine, I wouldn't want to live with a person who was always voicing ideas that I found unpleasant.

And yet . . .

Recently I met someone through an online dating site. His emails made it clear he was smart, nice, and forthcoming. Then there were his pictures: *far* too good to be true. (Except . . . there were a lot of them. And though he looked slightly different in all of them—more like Josh Hartnett in one, more like Matt Damon in another—the common denominator was handsomeness.) I decided meeting up was worth a shot. We agreed to get together to watch a soccer match at a local bar. When I arrived, I found he actually *did* look like the

young star in *Good Will Hunting* (if less broad and muscular). We sat on a big couch, eating a pub lunch, keeping an eye on the game, and chatting pleasantly. After about an hour, he suddenly put his arm around me and gave me a squeeze; I was simultaneously taken aback and charmed. Later we walked along the Brooklyn waterfront. When a summer storm broke out, we ran for cover under a tree—and he kissed me! Nonetheless, I wasn't sure how into it I was, for reasons I'll expand upon below. But when he asked me out for a second date, I figured, "Why not?" And when the question of Date #3 came up, I figured there was no harm in having another enjoyable dinner with him. And so it went . . . till we found ourselves agreeing not to see other people.

There was so much that I liked about him: his gentlemanliness, his generosity, his stability, his vast knowledge of just about everything (from classical philosophy to how to fix my broken food processor). Unfortunately, there was a lot I didn't like, too—and not just that he wasn't a terribly good listener. (As I learned from Jack's chapter on "Infinite Gesticulating," some men talk too much simply because they're nervous; not all of them are narcissists who don't let you get a word in edgewise because they think you have nothing worthwhile to say. Indeed, Good Will eventually began to notice when I opened my mouth—even if it wasn't till Date #4.) He had no interest in many of the things that I find most fun to think about, like modern art and poetry. And he'd spend just about every night drinking beers with his pals, if he could. My preferred form of social engagement was the dinner party—and I need vastly more downtime than he does.

A far bigger problem came in the form of his discourse on contemporary America. His politics aggravated me. He raved a little too often about how ideal it would be if states like New York and Vermont seceded from the rest of the country, complained a little too much about how much the government sucked without attempting to engender any productive solutions or proactive responses. One day I

got so irritated that I maturely exclaimed, "Okay, so everything sucks! I get it! But do you always need to point out so many new examples of the terribleness?"

Why, I wanted to know, did he waste so much of his time (and, um, mine?) complaining and suggesting impossible "solutions" to our nation's problems? Could I ever seriously date a man who so frequently annoyed me when we discussed the state of the world? Whom I often thought was mildly nuts? (I mean, really: Seceding from the union? Come on! It's never going to happen!)

But . . . Good Will was *so* very good to me. After years of poor treatment at the hands of New York's endless scalawags, and neglect from innumerable aspiring artist types (punishment that was, admittedly, somewhat self-inflicted), I breathed a sigh of relief to be with a man whose fondness for me was so transparent. He treated me as regally as I think we all (in our heart of hearts) want to be treated and was *always* there when I needed him. Like the wintery midnight when, after realizing I needed to dig my car out of the snow to avoid a morning ticket, I locked my keys into the damn thing . . . while it was running, as the flakes continued to fall, when I was freezing in a pair of gym shorts—and I didn't even have my wallet on me, or a pair of gloves. Then there was the day I fried my new laptop completely by spilling an entire cup of tea on it—while on deadline for this book!—followed up by the afternoon I got it back from the repair shop after spending seven hundred dollars to get it fixed . . . only to have it die again immediately. Or the week when I went through a major professional trauma and feared my career was over. He was there for me every time: biking over to wait with me for the locksmith, lending me his spare MacBook, advising me on what to do, and providing the emotional support that helped me to realize these things were molehills, not mountains.

And, sure, he wasn't terribly interested in chamber music performances at the Met—but he'd taken me to one and sat through

the second avant-garde half of the concert even though he hated it. He didn't really enjoy spending hours discussing movies after seeing them—but he'd come to the cinema with me and my friends and good-humoredly go along with our chats over dinner afterward. He hated talking on the phone (and admittedly, I kind of do, too), but when I made it clear that I liked saying a quick "Good night, sweet dreams" before I went to bed, he relented, and came to enjoy those moments himself.

But . . . the politics didn't stop annoying me. Bringing him into certain social situations (like, um, all of them) could be nerve-racking given how different his worldview was from that of most people I hung out with, and how eager he was to tell everyone his opinions. I didn't stop being disappointed by the limits imposed by our lack of overlapping interests.

Could this thing really continue much longer, let alone go the distance?

A few months after we met, I began reading E. M. Forster's masterpiece, the carefully plotted *Howards End*. It orbits around the Schlegel girls—two clever and cultured sisters of marrying age who become deeply involved with another London family, thanks to a few twists of fate. Helen, the younger and prettier of the Schlegels, is an idealist who doesn't like to compromise—not on her politics and not in relationships either. (Reading between the lines, I imagine that her great beauty probably encouraged her obstinacy: When you're a head turner, you don't learn how to be flexible in your youth, because everyone is so enamored that they bend to *your* will.) Down-to-earth Margaret more instinctually appreciates that there's a difference between what would be nice in an ideal world and what will make you happy in the real one. When Margaret—the sister I will focus on here—eventually meets a Good Will of her own, she must answer questions like those I find myself up against: Can a woman marry a man whose outlook on life is so different from her own? *Should* she?

As the book begins, Margaret, nearing thirty, seems headed for a life of spinsterdom (while twenty-year-old Helen doesn't seem to have much trouble getting into one dalliance after the other). The sisters socialize with a group of London intellectuals who believe that "affectionate personal relations and the contemplation of beauty are the supremely good states of mind," as David Lodge puts it in his introduction to the Penguin classic edition. The girls and their pals keep up on all the latest cultural events; they pore over all the new ideas; they read in part because it helps them to have better conversations, and they converse in part because it helps them enjoy their reading more. The well-educated Schlegels are suffragists who want to change the world. They do what they can for their less fortunate friends. Their ethical ideals are closely linked to their aesthetic ideas: Justice helps keep the world orderly, and beautiful. If the book were set in today's America, the Schlegels would be New York City liberals.

While vacationing in Germany, the sisters meet some fellow Britons, the Wilcoxes—the equivalent of modern-day Republicans. The most Wilcoxian of them all is the paterfamilias, Henry, a no-nonsense capitalist and rubber baron. Though he's not a bad guy, he doesn't think much about how his business practices affect anyone but himself, his associates, and his (narrowly defined) family. He and the other Wilcoxes are focused on what Margaret calls "the outer life"—of practical details and tangible accomplishments—rather than the inner life of emotional discoveries and the psychological pleasure of ideas that don't really have any "use." The Wilcoxes—bourgeois, philistine, stereotypically male—are competitors, always out to find the advantage in order to win.

Despite their differences, the two families are drawn to each other. Helen and Mr. Wilcox's younger son, Paul, have a fling—but when it ends unhappily, she begins to disdain him and his relatives. Margaret, on the other hand, recognizes that the Wilcox approach is more practical than her own, much as she finds it distasteful. "It does

breed character," she muses, during a conversation with her sister. She admires the way Mr. Wilcox has "his hands on all the ropes"— which I took to mean that he sure knows how to sail the boat of life. She begins to recognize the importance of what she calls "proportion"—that is, compromise. As she says to a new friend at one point, a person should always start out with the highest of ideals, but "proportion [should] come in as a last resource, when the better things have failed, and a deadlock [would otherwise set in]." Margaret is so interested in finding common ground that she's responsible for one of the most popular catchphrases in all of literature: "Only connect"!

Margaret and the widowed Mr. Wilcox forge an unexpected camaraderie. Henry is many years her senior, but she's charmed by his confidence and competence—two of the qualities I liked so much in Good Will. Henry, in turn, respects Margaret for being strong-willed but not stubborn and takes comfort in her kindness. When he proposes to her, she's surprised—she doesn't consider herself a "catch" and he is, after all, a wealthy tycoon. At the same time, she's delighted: "An immense joy came over her [that] most resembled the all-pervading happiness of fine weather." She becomes preoccupied with the idea that Henry loves her—which helps her begin to love him in return. So—to Helen's great displeasure—Margaret agrees to be his wife and hopes she can make Henry a better and happier man with her love.

But will she really be able to pull anything like that off?

After the two of them go through serious trials together—one of Margaret's relatives becomes unexpectedly pregnant, out of wedlock, and one of Henry's is charged with homicide—Margaret *does* help to transform Henry significantly. His difficulties—and respectful love for her—enlighten him to the importance of empathy. Their relationship becomes the basis for a small utopia: They move to a home called Howards End with some members of their newly combined family. As Margaret seems to understand intuitively, and

Henry eventually appreciates himself, a happy society—and a happy couple—isn't made out of rigid conformity to certain ideas, but by compromising within the bounds of a moral framework.

So . . . will Good Will and I last? I'm not sure, but I can't help but keep Margaret in mind as I puzzle it out. She intuited that a romantic alliance based on mutual trust and affection can be transcendent and transformative, and that having a partner who concerns himself chiefly with being a provider and a protector—the way both Good Will and Henry do—isn't necessarily a bad thing. Maybe someone who's more interested in the details of the outer life is *exactly* whom I need to be with, considering that I'm a bit of a dreamer and a bohemian myself, not unlike Margaret when she first met Henry. Maybe Good Will can provide the architecture, so to speak, and I can handle the interior decorating.

It sounds like a pretty good recipe for a home sweet home, doesn't it?

MISTAKEN LONELYHEARTS?
Trust Us—Advice Columnists
Don't Know Everything

As Jack and I near the end of our book, I think it's worth mentioning a fictional character who is about as similar to us, professionally, as they come: the advice columnist Miss Lonelyhearts.

The antihero of Nathanael West's eponymous dark classic, Lonelyhearts—who is a man, despite his feminine nom de plume—tries to give readers words of wisdom that will help them through their personal difficulties, as we've tried to do within these pages. But ironically, the longer Lonelyhearts writes his column, the less effective as a counselor he becomes. Though he's paid to essentially dole out expertise on how to live a happy life, doing so pushes Lonelyhearts slowly but surely toward a nervous breakdown—in part because the letters he receives from his readers remind him incessantly of how much suffering and despair there is in the world.

Lonelyhearts took on the columnist job, despite the fact that he knew it was "a circulation stunt and the whole staff [considered] it a joke," because he'd hoped the new gig would lead to bigger and better things. But after several months of being earnestly entreated for help by Depression-era letter writers trying to cope with problems like domestic abuse, disfigurement, and, of course, abject poverty, Lonelyhearts can no longer take his position lightly. "He sees that

the majority of the letters are profoundly humble pleas for moral and spiritual advice, that they are . . . expressions of genuine suffering," as he puts it (describing himself in the third person to his on-again, off-again girlfriend Betty). "He also discovers that his correspondents take him seriously."

Lonelyhearts, a New England puritan and the son of a Baptist minister, wishes he could assure his readers that there's a reason to keep living, but he's having trouble seeing the point himself. Much as he'd like to tell them to keep the faith, he doesn't know how to convince them that they should. Much as he'd like to believe in Jesus Christ, he doesn't. Much as he'd like to become Christlike himself, it's difficult for him to overcome his hopelessness enough to be a Dear Abby, let alone a charismatic spiritual leader. He considers passing on to his readers some advice from Father Zossima, that character in *The Brothers Karamazov*, a novel he keeps by his bed: "Love a man even in his sin, for that is the semblance of Divine Love and is the highest love on earth. . . . Love all God's creation, the whole and every grain of sand in it. Love the animals, love the plants, love everything. If you love everything, you will perceive the divine mystery in things. Once you perceive it, you will begin to comprehend it better every day. And you will come at last to love the whole world with an all embracing love."

It's a gorgeous approach, really—but Lonelyhearts can't pay it forward, because he has trouble adhering to it. Much as he wants to help his followers—who are, in the main, abstractions to him, "visible" to him only through their letters—he doesn't seem to like real, live human beings all that much. Tormented soul that he is, he's barely capable of loving the woman he cares about most in life— gentle Betty. Though he proposes to her shortly before his break- down really kicks in, he begins avoiding her the very day after she agrees to marry him, annoyed that she'd fooled him (or he'd fooled himself) "into thinking that such a solution was possible."

For a brief period, as a young man, Lonelyhearts had been able to believe in certain things: "in literature . . . in Beauty and in personal expression as an absolute end." But when those bulwarks fail him, he can't find acceptable organizing principles to replace them. It's not only increasingly impossible for him to work; it's harder and harder for him to feel at peace in the world. When Betty hears that he's been calling in sick to work, she encourages him to quit. But as he tells her, resigning won't help. He sees no real way out. Even if he ditched the job, he'd never be able to forget the letters.

As is probably clear to you by now, Lonelyhearts is severely depressed—and much as he strives to be a good person, his cynicism has worn him down so severely that he struggles more and more with his basest instincts. He flirts with his boss's wife, sleeps with a woman married to a crippled man, and attacks an old gay gent in a bar, twisting the guy's arm with such determination that the man begins to scream. By the end of the book, Lonelyhearts is so sick in the head that he enters into a manic fit, and it's only in his delusional state that he finally begins to believe. He fancies that he is in communication with God. Thinking God wants him to heal the aforementioned handicapped cuckold by hugging him, Lonelyhearts complies. The slight problem is that the other man happens to be armed with a loaded weapon.

I bring up *Miss Lonelyhearts* not simply because I want to suggest that embracing an armed man may not be the wisest of ideas, but more to underscore what you may have already concluded on your own: Professional advice givers though we may be, Jack and I are also, at times, slightly screwed up, occasionally confused, and not infrequently depressed ourselves. But unlike Lonelyhearts when he began, we've been quite serious from the minute we started this project about wanting to do right by you, and neither one of us was on the verge of a nervous breakdown while we were writing.

At different points in our lives, Jack and I have searched as desperately as Lonelyhearts for meaning. A lot of the time, we have found it

in stories: the fictional ones we read, the true ones we tell each other, and the order-giving narratives we construct for our own lives. We haven't quite achieved Happily Ever After just yet. But unlike Lonely-hearts, we believe in many things: great literature, personal expression, and close friendships. Beauty, truth, humanity: All of those things help us to understand how we're connected to the larger world.

Poor Lonelyhearts seemed to think that meaning in life could be attained by way of a formula, that if only he could convince himself, during some kind of eureka moment, to believe in this simple thing or that, quotidian existence would be easy. On the contrary, meaning is something we have to work to find and reaffirm on a daily basis. But once we get into the habit of looking for the meaning, listening for the narrative, remaining alert for the beauty, and striving to con-nect, the work isn't hard; in fact, there's a strange pleasure in it.

It's one of those funny paradoxes: If you don't believe in meaning, you'll never look for it, which means you'll never find it. Something similar could be said about love.

"Only connect," Forster said.

To which I want to say, *Only? Only! Buddy, do you know how hard that is?* But maybe it's not quite as hard as we think.

ACKNOWLEDGMENTS

From Jack

Gratitude can never be expressed adequately, but to get started, I'd like to thank my agent, Richard Abate, and Danica Mitrovic, my host in Serbia where I did much of the first draft (*cmok, cmok*). I'd like to thank our original editor, Amber Qureshi, and our ultimate editor, Leah Miller, for their help and enthusiasm. I'd like to thank Maura for suggesting the idea for the book (and for all her hard, excellent work) and dear Dave Kaufman for introducing me to Maura in the first place. And I'd like to thank Sarah Harrison, who, time and again, sustained me.

From Maura

There are so many people whom I acknowledge in my heart on a regular basis; if only I could name them all here. But I will try to keep this brief . . . Without you, Kate Taylor, I'm not sure I would've gotten through the last few years, to say nothing of finishing this book. Teddy Wayne, your support and advice means a lot to me. Prem Krishnamurthy, you were a special help with this endeavor. Mary Catherine Siebel, *il miglior* advice-giver, I adore you. You too, Zac Frank. Tim Sheehy, you have helped me through so many breakups that I'll be forever indebted. Jason Stem, you will always be a part of me. I'm grateful to you, Adrienne Brodeur and Dan Menaker, for all you've done to encourage me over the years; to you, Tom Beller and Suzy Hansen, for helping launch me as an essay writer. Alison Brower, Abby Pesta, Denise Brodey, Pam O'Brien, and Nanette Varian: thank

you for the professional support—and the assignments! Wayne Johnston, Pinckney Benedict, and Courtney Brkic, your writerly advice has been invaluable. I chant the phrase "Kate Lee, agent extraordinaire," whenever I need a confidence boost—I appreciate you so much, you smart, hard-working advocate, you. In my retirement years I hope to be hanging out up north with my editor Leah Miller, making jam and painting pictures with the other old ladies. (Amber Qureshi, please join us up there!) Jocelyn Kalmus, stalwart publicist, I'm so impressed by all your hard work—and your amazing spread sheets! Jack, your love of literature helped spawn this book; your wit and wisdom made it fun. Evan Vetere, you have brightened up my life. Finally, I thank my sister and especially my father, for his love . . . though I really hope he doesn't read this book! At least not chapter 8.

ABOUT THE AUTHORS

Jack Murnighan has a PhD in medieval and renaissance literature from Duke University. His most recent book, *Beowulf on the Beach: What to Love and What to Skip in Literature's 50 Greatest Hits,* helped tens of thousands of readers rediscover their love of the classics. His two previous books, *The Naughty Bits* and *Classic Nasty,* were critically acclaimed tours of sexuality in the history of literature, providing spirited essays on and excerpts of more than seventy-five authors each. He appears frequently on NPR and has written about relationships and sexuality for a variety of magazines, including *Esquire, Glamour,* and *Nerve,* and currently writes the advice column "Male Take" for YourTango.com. He was the co-editor of *Full Frontal Fiction* and has had essays and short stories appear in eleven anthologies. He worked as the editor-in-chief of Nerve.com and now is the director of content of Babble.com. He lives in New York City.

Maura Kelly was a staff writer for *Glamour,* a relationships columnist for *amNew York,* and a dating blogger for *Marie Claire.* Her personal essays, opinion pieces, and reportage have appeared in three literary anthologies and in publications including *The New York Times, The Washington Post, The Boston Globe, Salon, Slate, The Daily Beast, The Believer, The Guardian,* and *Rolling Stone.* She received her BA in psychology from Dartmouth College and her MFA in creative writing after studying at Hollins and George Mason Universities.